D0121455

# THE WOODS BELONG TO ME

# THE WOODS BELONG TO ME

## A Gamekeeper's Life

**ANGUS NUDDS**
EDITED BY JOHN HUMPHREYS

ILLUSTRATED BY
WILLIAM GARFIT

BLANDFORD PRESS
POOLE • DORSET

First published in the UK 1985 by Blandford Press,
Link House, West Street, Poole, Dorset, BH15 1LL.

Distributed in the United States by
Sterling Publishing Co., Inc.,
2 Park Avenue, New York, N.Y. 10016

ISBN 0 7137 1659 2

**British Library Cataloguing in Publication Data**

Nudds, Angus
   The woods belong to me : a gamekeeper's life.
   1. Nudds, Angus   2. Gamekeepers—England—
   Biography
   I. Title   II. Humphreys, John, 1939-
   639.9′5′0924          SK354.N8

   ISBN 0-7137-1659-2

Typeset by Graphicraft Typesetters Ltd., Hong Kong
Printed in Great Britain by
Butler & Tanner Ltd, Frome and London

TO MY WIFE AUDREY,
SOMEONE SPECIAL

# Contents

# Foreword

During the forty years since the last War, my wife and I have been lucky enough to have employed many people at Tetworth with whom we have had special friendly relationships. It would be no reflection on those friendships if I say that Angus Nudds, apart from his unrivalled expertise in his craft and ability to pass on his knowledge to others, and to endear himself to my guests, tenants and neighbours, has been a real friend and advisor of whom I can ask advice on all problems of country life. On my side, I think I have been able to enthuse him with the delights of other country sports – hunting and fishing. He is also, of course, a very good golfer and shot.

When I telephoned Angus's previous employer, Sammy Christie-Miller (whom I had known in the Cavalry Division during the War) and asked him to give Angus a reference, he simply said, 'Don't miss him'. He was right.

I hope everyone who enjoys country life will read this book, not only for its knowledge but also for its delightful natural expression. To me it is something really special.

Sir Peter Crossman
*Tetworth Hall, 1985*

# 1 · Boyhood

When I look back over my life, I was, from a very early age, destined to become a gamekeeper or to be connected with nature in some way or another. I was born and raised in that lovely little fishing village on the north Norfolk coast, Brancaster Staithe, in the days when it really was a fishing village and not a collection of holiday homes, as it is now. The whole of my boyhood was spent wandering in thousands of acres of saltings and marshes in pursuit of, or just watching, the many species of ducks and waders that congregated there. The

famous bird sanctuary, Scolt Head, lies at the entrance of Brancaster Staithe harbour and many different kinds of migratory birds rest along that particular stretch of coastline.

Charles Chestney was the warden on Scolt Head and his job was to look after the large colony of Sandwich, common and little terns that nested there every year. The terns were treated more like old friends by the fishermen and they took great delight in being the first to see them arrive each year and casually saying, 'I see the old terns are here'. The terns arrived at about the same time as the Brent geese departed, in late March or early April. When the Brent geese are preparing to go to their nesting grounds, they become very restless. Before they feel the migratory urge, they feed quite happily for long periods but now they spend much of their day flying in large numbers up and down the harbour, calling very loudly to one another. These flights are to get themselves fit for their long journey to the Arctic regions and their nesting grounds. A week or so before they depart, every time they take wing, they usually head due north for a mile or so and later return and start feeding again.

They fly further and further north each time until they eventually disappear and, the next day, the harbour seems strangely quiet without them. This is something that I have witnessed for many years and, to this day, I still find it fascinating. The power of nature is a wonderful thing, when one reflects that migratory birds are still doing from instinct what their ancestors have done for thousands of years! The old birds teach their young but it is pure instinct and their powers of navigation are still not wholly understood.

My great pal in those days was Bob Chestney, son of the warden, and together we spent most of our free time, when we were not at school, either with Bob's father on Scolt Head or out on the marshes and many a feeding redshank or curlew was rudely disturbed by either the loud plop of a stone from our catapults or a homemade arrow from one of our bows quivering in the mud close beside it. I do not remember ever actually hitting one, but we always went out with great enthusiasm. We knew all the likely places where the waders fed and used the small creeks to conceal our approach until we were in range and near enough to let fly. This taught us fieldcraft, a skill which was to become very useful to both of us in later life. The strange thing is that, although we spend hours and hours trying to crawl within range of the redshanks and the curlew, two of the most wary birds on the marsh, we never dreamed of firing at the many stints, which were so tame that they actually ran over the fishermen's boots in search of food when the fishermen were musseling. Looking back on it now, we would probably have stopped a seaboot with our backsides if ever we had shot an arrow at them.

Billy Daniels, the local gamekeeper, allowed us to go into the

woods to cut hazel rods to make our bows from and we brought home some of the bamboo that was often washed up on the tide line. When these were split down and sandpapered, they made very fine arrows and, if we bound a small nail onto one end, they would fly much further. The next step was to make our arrows fly straighter, so we needed some flight feathers; we looked no further than my mother's very large Plymouth rock cockerel.

I'll swear that old rooster knew when we were making arrows because, when we were engaged in splitting and sandpapering our bamboos, he would be quite happy out in the open orchard with his wives scratching away and clucking peacefully. When we came to the part when we needed the flight feathers, and stealthily crept out of the back door to catch the old rooster, he was nowhere to be seen.

Another one of our winter activities was going out at night around the farmers' corn stacks, ratting with the aid of a torch and a stick! I found a golf club the best weapon, which may be why I took up golf later in life. There were many corn stacks in those days before the coming of the combine harvester and we used to plan our outings in order to visit about four stacks each night, giving us something to do every evening of the week. As we approached the corn stacks, we could hear the rats squeaking and rustling; when we switched on our torches, they would run along the runs they had made and then we had quite a hectic time killing them as fast as we could. Sometimes a rat would

jump from the stacks and onto our shoulders and then onto the ground to try to make an escape, quite a frightening experience.

We killed great numbers of rats each year, for which the farmers were so grateful they gave us a few coppers to help buy the batteries for our torches. One night, when we were rat-catching, I fell over something stuck in the ground; on close inspection, we found it was a 'bender' that had been set by the keepers to snare some of the rats. When a rat ran into the snare, it triggered the bent hazel rod which straightened, lifting the rat off the ground in such a way that he was unable to bite through the snare cord. We examined this device most carefully and, a few days later, had our own 'benders' set. I hate to think how many times we had to release the next-door neighbour's cat!

In those days, our lives were split into seasons and things have not changed much today. Once the end of February came, we would hang up our catapults and bows and our thoughts turned to bird's nesting. We never ever took any eggs, Bob's father saw to that, but just took simple delight in finding them. We spent a lot of time on the Common looking for shelduck nests. The shelduck is a handsome bird which nests in the many rabbit holes on the Common. When we found a nest, we kept a watchful eye on it until the eggs hatched. Then we counted the infertile eggs and reported the event to Bob's father. A newly-hatched shelduck brood is one of the loveliest sights one could wish to see. Early in the morning, the parent birds escort the brood a mile or so down the Common lane to the marshes. If any danger, such as a human being or any other predator appeared, the old birds would take wing and the ducklings would scatter in all directions. The parent birds would become agitated and try to draw the cause of danger away from their young by pretending to have a broken wing or be hurt in some way or another.

When the old birds were satisfied that danger no longer threatened, they would gather their young and continue their journey to the marshes. Once they had brought the ducklings safely to the marsh, they set about the task of rearing them. When the young are about three-quarters grown a strange thing happens; several pairs of old birds will gather all their broods together and then fly off and leave their young in charge of just two adults. I have seen as many as sixty young being looked after by only two adults. I do not know where the old birds go to, as they leave the harbour completely, but I suspect they hide away somewhere safe to shed their flight feathers because most species of duck and geese are unable to fly when they are in the process of moulting.

Some days, when he was not too busy with the many people who visited Scolt Head, Bob's father would take us with him and show us round the ternery. You had to be careful where you put your feet as the nests were so thick on the sands. We were also allowed to go in search of the nests of oystercatcher, skylark, redshank and the other brids that nested there. Very often, on our way home, we would stop to gather winkles, cockles or samphire, according to the time of year, or make a special trip down the harbour to go 'butt-pricking'. This involved having a long-handled fork with about six barbed tines on it; the butts, a local name for dabs, would cover themselves with sand and lie in fairly shallow water in the sun. Wearing only a pair of swimming turnks, we would wade through the pools and shallows when the tide was out, stabbing the sand as we went and every now and again we would get a fish. This was not only a great sport but also a very welcome source of food during the war years when most things were rationed.

Life in Brancaster Staithe in those days revolved around the sea; there were many things to be done when the tide was in, whilst other things had to wait until low water. I remember how good the fishermen were with us boys, how they taught and encouraged us to think for ourselves. Sometimes of an evening, when the tide was in and they were busy boiling the whelks they had caught that day, they would give us some of their whelks and a piece of string and ask us to try to catch some swinners (marsh crabs) for them to use as bait in their whelk pots for the next day.

Off we would go to the quay where there were thousands of swinners that lived in between the bricks that made up the wall of the quay. As one would expect, the bigger boys grabbed the best places and caught the most but, when we took our catch to the fishermen, they always found one or two swinners in the small boys' catch equally valuable as those from bigger boys so we would all finish up with a penny each. Later on in life, after the war, when my brother started fishing for whelks, I found out from him that the swinners were not as good for bait as we had been led to believe: I suppose what had really happened was that we were kept out of mischief for an hour or two. When I go back home during the summer months, to this day I see small boys swinner-catching in exactly the same places as I did and no doubt being as nicely conned as I was but, of course, I never let on.

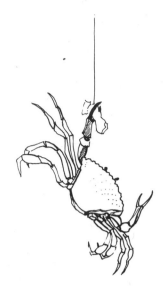

One of the highlights of our lives at that time was the Regatta held every August at Brancaster Staithe: rowing, sailing, tub and shovel, swimming races and a greasy pole fixed out over the water in the quay. There were cash prizes for the winners and naturally we entered everything we could, eager to try and win some money to spend at the fair, held at night on the Jolly Sailors' field. We were very well behaved during the weeks before the Regatta, having being threatened with not being allowed to go if we misbehaved, and we were always on the lookout for ways to earn money to spend at the fair.

One day, about a month before the Regatta, Mr Adams and his wife, who lived at Brancaster Hall, asked Bob and me if we would collect all the old tins and bottles out of the creek in front of the Sailing Club, so that the boats might be launched without people cutting their feet on rusty tins. The part that interested us most was the opportunity to earn some money, so we completed this task in a very short space of time. The next time we saw Mr and Mrs Adams they thanked us very much for doing a good job but, as they had no money with them, they promised to pay us later. For the next two or three weeks, whenever they came to the Sailing Club, we always made ourselves very conspicuous but, no luck, and, by the time of the Regatta, we had given up all hopes of being paid. After the event, we had to go home and clean ourselves and have a meal but we were back at the fair almost immediately. After an hour or so, when we had run out of money, the house party from Brancaster Hall arrived at the fairground and Mr Adams came over to us, announced that he had never paid us for cleaning those tins from the creek and gave us a crisp £1 note each, which in those days was a small fortune.

Away we went again on the dodgems and the swing-boats and stuffed ourselves with Mrs Gizzie's home-made rock. Before very long we were broke once more and reduced to scanning the ground to see if we could find any money that might have been dropped. Later in the day, Mrs Adams met us and said, 'Angus and Bobby; now let me see, we never paid you for clearing those tins out of the creek', and she gave us another £1 note each. As you might expect, we said thank you very much and went off and spent the lot. I had the pleasure of telling this story to Mr Adams about five years ago and he found it very amusing but, being the gentleman that he is, he would not take his £1 note back again but insisted on buying me a large scotch instead!

Until I was about nine or ten, we lived next door to Jimmy Clark, the village blacksmith. His forge was the meeting point for all the older men and the retired fishermen. Several of them, including my father, had been members of the crew of the Brancaster lifeboat, which was taken out of service because of the difficulty in launching her. She was launched by means of horses, which had to come from the farms in the village over one mile away. I loved sitting quietly in the corner of the shop listening to their stories of the days gone by, of how they used to row and sail the whelk boats out to the fishing grounds. They certainly worked hard in those days, for the ropes attached to the whelk pots were hauled by hand, whereas today they not only have much bigger and more powerful boats to travel out to the fishing grounds, but also mechanical haulers to do the heavy work. The whelk boats of today are decked with wheelhouses to give some protection from the weather but,

when my father went to sea, the boats were not nearly as big and were not decked, so that the crew were exposed to the elements for up to sixteen hours a day.

They were a very brave breed of men and, when I see the modern boats riding a rough sea, being tossed about like corks in a mill race, I wonder how the men and boats of years ago ever survived. I have seen my father come in from sea in the winter time with his hands bleeding due to hand-hauling ropes, which, rough and hard at the best of times, froze as they came out of the water. In those days, I never understood why, when the weather turned unexpectedly rough and the whelk boats were still out at sea, mother became rather short-tempered and we kids had to be on our best behaviour. She would gaze anxiously out of the back window which overlooked the harbour. As soon as she saw the whelk boats appear round the point she became a different person, busy getting father's meal ready. She had things timed very well. As soon as the boats rounded the point, mother put the vegetables on to cook and the meal would be ready the moment father walked through the door. I feel it was always worse for those people on the shore, not knowing what's going on and worrying if their menfolk were going to get home safely.

When Mr Clark had several wagon- or cartwheels to 'shoe' he usually asked us lads to help; we were very keen because it meant the fun of having a big bonfire. Firstly the process involved cranking strips of iron through a machine which consisted of a set of cogwheels, rollers and a handle. As the iron came through the machine, it was slowly bent into a circle, the diameter being determined by adjustment of the cogwheel. The tyre was then taken into the forge to have the two ends welded together; they were heated in the fire until they were white hot, then quickly taken out and hammered on the anvil. When the weld was finished, it was not easy to see where it had been joined. The next job was to heat the whole tyre in a bonfire of sticks and brush wood; this made the metal expand. The wheel was laid on a circular piece of metal with a large hole in the centre, which fitted the hub. As soon as the tyre reached the correct temperature it was hammered onto the wheel and water was poured over it to cool it and shrink it on to the wheel. Whenever we saw any broken wheels being unloaded in the blacksmith's yard, we had difficulty in containing ourselves until it was time to put the new tyres on them. The blacksmith waited until several wheels needed 'shoeing' so that he could make most use of the one bonfire.

Jimmy Clark was also a very talented man in wrought iron-work, a lovely example of which may be seen today where the nave of the church meets the chancel in the church at Burnham Deepdale. I remember clearly watching him hammer out the delicate petals of the flowers and fitting them all together; he had bits and pieces strewn all over the floor of his shop. Firstly he made drawings in chalk on the floor, then, when he had finished a particular piece, it was placed on the drawing in its final position and woe betide anyone who accidentally kicked one of the sections out of place. After he had made all the parts, they were welded or riveted together to become a real work of art and it was a marvel how those big hands, that looked so clumsy when they were welding a big hammer, could create such delicate work.

When our family grew larger, and I was ten or eleven years old, we moved to the old White Horse public house. Bullards, the brewers, had built the new public house and my father was

given a chance to rent the old place. We quickly recognised it as a boys' paradise, for there were ten rooms in the house, two sets of bedroom stairs, four different doors to run through and an enormous cellar where the barrels of beer had been kept, and which boasted another separate entrance down which the barrels slid. Outside was a range of stables and loose boxes, haylofts and a pigeon loft, the perfect place for boys, as on fine days we could be out on the marsh and on wet days we played in the stables. The large garden ran down to the saltings so that, on warm summer evenings, we were able to run to the bottom of the garden and swim in the creek when the tide was in. During the war, tame rabbits made a lot of money so it was not long before all the stables and loose boxes were full of rabbits. We had hundreds; even the Andersen air-raid shelter that the Council made us dig into the garden was full of them so that, had there been an air raid or an invasion, at least the rabbits would have been safe. A large slice of our time was spent in obtaining food for them and I am afraid many of the farmers' swede and turnip fields were raided at night to feed those hungry mouths.

Every Boxing Day, most of the men and boys of the village gathered in the morning to have a day's rabbiting on the Common, a hundred acres of land covered in gorse and bracken, among which lived thousands of rabbits. The Hall Farm had the sporting rights over the Common but, on Boxing Day, the folk who lived in the village were allowed to catch as many as they wanted. We always met in the Jolly Sailors' yard at about half past seven in the morning; someone would bring along a handcart on which were loaded several gallon jars of beer, which obviously had to be sampled to make sure that my grandfather, who kept the Jolly Sailors, had drawn it from the barrel correctly and it was fit to drink. When the beer was safely aboard, on went our nets, some proper rabbit nets but mostly old fishing nets that had seen better days. The fact that the mesh was a bit rotten did not matter very much.

The cart was then pulled up the Common lane, accompanied by up to twenty men and boys and numerous dogs of all shapes, sizes and breeds. Every breed of dog in the country and quite a few combinations were represented there. When we arrived on the Common, we were met by Billy Daniels, the gamekeeper, who was in charge of the day's sport. The beer had to be sampled again to make sure it had travelled well, all very frustrating for us lads who wanted to get on with the more serious business of rabbiting! Eventually the nets were set along the grass rides between areas of gorse bushes and bracken; Billy Daniels had smoked the rabbits out from their holes a few days before in preparation for our big day. We walked through the bushes and bracken, driving rabbits into the nets, although what usually happened was that a rabbit, pursued by several dogs, would be started straight for the nets but, at the last second, the bunny would make a sharp turn and avoid it, while the dogs carried straight on and into it. This beating of the bushes and bracken was thirsty work so several trips had to be made by the men to the handcart to quench their thirst and, as the day wore on, we not only caught rabbits and dogs in the nets but quite a few of the men as well. We usually managed to get enough rabbits to justify going again next year and everyone, including the dogs, went home happy and tired, some rather unsteadily, but it did not matter, it was downhill all the way and the Jolly Sailors was at the bottom of the Common lane.

Old Herbert Winterboon (known as Rock-bottom), who lived next door to us, was a retired fisherman who did not enjoy the best of health in his later years but he took an interest in my brother and me and taught us quite a few things about the sea and the fishing. On summer evenings, if he was feeling well, he would get us to row or sail him around the harbour, teaching us to row double oars, himself sitting in the stern, beating out the stroke with his walking stick. He also taught us where to find the best samphire and the biggest winkles and how the butts or dabs follow the tide up the creeks, feeding as they go, and then drop back into the deeper water as the tide goes out. He showed us  the best creeks for fish and went with us in the boat to set the net across the mouth of the river just as the tide turned. We then rowed him home and we lads walked back when the tide had gone out and collected the fish caught in the net.

Like most fishermen, Herbert would be guided in his judgement by the wind and would never go fishing when it blew from the east. He used to say, when the wind blew from the east, that 'It's neither good for man nor beast', and he was absolutely right. Many is the time I have tried fishing in an east wind but seldom have I had a good day. When we went shrimping, we would pull the trawl up and down the beach, chest-deep in the water, and he would sit on an upturned bait box on the shore and sort out the shrimps from the weed and other foreign bodies. The shrimps were taken home and cooked in boiling sea water in a copper. If they are cooked in that way, they taste much better than those boiled in tap water.

Another method of catching fish which he taught us was to

set a short net across the bottom or ebb tide end of the holes in the harbour; there were several of these deep 'pots' left after the tide had gone out and they all had names: Jone's Hole, Tom Winterboon's Hole, Norton Hole and so on. When the net was set, we used to row the boat up to the head of the hole and start to beat the water with a long pole. The end of the pole was shod with iron, to which was attached iron rings and these jingled when the pole hit the water and again when it sank and was moved about on the bottom. One of us would beat while the other slowly rowed the boat back and forth across the hole, with Herbert directing operations from the stern. Gradually, we worked our way towards the net, frightening the fish before us. It was especially exciting when it was time to haul in and see what we had caught. I suppose, in a way, we each benefited for we lads learnt a great deal from Herbert Winterboon and he in turn would not have been able to have enjoyed those extra days down at the harbour if we had not rowed him in his boat.

My father and several of the other men in the village played golf on the Royal West Norfolk Golf Course at Brancaster. There was a very strong Artisan Club in Brancaster and Brancaster Staithe and great rivalry between the men of each village. Perhaps it was hearing my father and his friends talking of their Sunday morning games, coupled with the fact that there were quite a few old hickory-shafted golf clubs around the house, that started me playing the game. We were given the clubs but had to find our own golf balls, which we did by walking across the harbour when the tide was out and searching among the marram grass and bushes along the seventh, eighth and ninth holes on the golf course for any balls that had been lost by the members.

When we had found enough we would start our game, but the village club members would not allow us to play on the Royal West Norfolk Course until we had learned to play and, more important, to behave properly. We were encouraged to play on the few holes that the men had made along the edge of the marsh on the west side of the village. The course was heavily grazed by horses, cattle and old Skipper's flock of geese, with the rabbits cropping what was left. Our parents could not afford to buy us proper golf shoes but the problem of slipping was solved by a visit to Geoff Ward, the village cobbler at Brancaster, who hammered some hob nails in the soles of our boots. His charge for this service was always the same, a pint of winkles, which we could gather for him from the harbour.

The first hole we played began with a most intimidating drive. The player stood on the edge of the village green and had to carry his ball over the creek on to the marsh; if he topped his drive, he lost the ball in the water when the tide was in, or buried it in the soft mud when the tide was out. If we hit a big slice backed by a south-westerly wind, we were in danger of hitting Lazarus Sands' house on the island or if we hit a snap hook, the ball would fly into Reggie Kendall's (the village butcher's) slaughterhouse. Perhaps this is why I have had a tendency to hook the ball all my life,, for I was more afraid of upsetting old Lazarus Sands than I was of hitting the slaughter-house. Reggie Kendall, the butcher, played golf and was always sympathetic towards the problem of keeping drives straight.

When we had safely negotiated the hazards of the first drive and arrived on the marsh fairway, the shot to the green had to be very accurate. The green was surrounded by dense gorse and bramble bushes which were absolutely impenetrable so, if we missed the green with our approach shot, it usually meant another lost ball. If we were lucky and landed our ball on the green, we had to clear a path through the rabbit droppings or remove a cow pat from the line of our putt and, very often, when we had struck the ball straight and true to the hole, it would deflect off a rabbit dropping which we had not seen. These golf holes ran along the Greenshore between the arable farm land on one side and the saltings on the other and many was the time we waited patiently for the tide to go out so that we could retrieve our last ball in order to continue the game. At the entrance to Brancaster Staithe harbour and running back along the beach towards Titchwell are the remains of an old petrified forest. You can still see clearly the outlines of the trees where they fell; they must have been massive specimens. This part of the old forest is known by the local people as The Scurves and many interesting fossils may be found there. I have seen a handsome pair of fossilised red deer antlers found in The Scurves. During the last fifteen years, the sea has eroded tons of sand so that now more and more of The Scurves are showing up at low tide. It is amazing how much a shoreline can change during one's own lifetime.

Over the years, the sea and the fishermen have made holes around the base of The Scurves into which the crabs move as the tide came in; when the tide turned and The Scurves showed above the water, we lads went to catch the crabs with the aid of a crab hook; a tool was easily made by begging an eighteen-inch length of small-diameter iron rod from Jimmy Clark, the blacksmith. He would make a small hook in one end and we attached this to a broomstick. The crab hook could then be pushed into the holes and you immediately knew if a crab was at home because you heard the iron hook grating on his shell. Then you slid the hook underneath the crab and hooked his claws, or sometimes he would grab the hook and thus be easily drawn from his hideout. Occasionally we had an extra stroke of luck and caught a lobster. If we did, we never ate it; we could not afford to for they were worth £1 each, which was a deal of money in those days. We carried a length of string with us to tie the lobster's claws so that he could not nip. It we put a lobster in a bag among the crabs without first tying his claws, he would very quickly chop the crabs to pieces. We spent many happy hours after the crabs and enjoyed eating them the next day. I think most things taste much nicer if you have caught or grown them yourself.

I was setting off on a crabbing expedition one day and was passing the golf clubhouse when Tom King, the professional, called me and asked if I would take a job caddying. He knew that I had never done this before and carefully explained what was required of me. He added that, for my pains, I would be paid one shilling which I must take home to my mother but, if I did my job well, I would get a sixpenny tip which I might keep. It was a new experience for me and I needed the money so I had a go and found that I enjoyed it. After about two months of this, Tom King must have had some good reports of me, because I was upgraded to the senior boy caddy with a pay rise to one shilling and sixpence per round and still the sixpenny tip.

A lady I caddied for often in those days was a Mrs Robarts from Thornham. She always brought along her grossly over-weight cocker spaniel dog, Rover, and I think the main reason she played golf was to give Rover his exercise. Mrs Robarts had a slight speech impediment, being unable to pronounce the letter 'R', so Rover became 'Wover'. When Mr and Mrs Robarts arrived on the first tee, I was handed Rover's lead with strict instructions that on no account was I to let him off because 'Wover' would go off in the sand dunes 'wabbitting'. At went well until we reached the short fourth hole which cuts across the course, close to the fifteenth tee behind which were the beach huts under which lived a colony of rabbits. I gave Mrs Robarts her driver and walked with Rover round the path at the bottom of the hill and the fourth tee. Arthur Overson, who was caddying for Mr Robarts and me, had nearly rounded the hill when Rover, who did not care to leave his mistress too far behind, sat down and refused to budge. I gave his lead a mighty tug and his collar came off over his head. As soon as the dog realised he was free, he made a beeline for the beach huts and the

rabbits. I explained what had happened to Mrs Robarts who said, 'Naughty Wover; he often does that; we will play the hole out and then go and find him.'

It was quite easy to find him because, when we arrived at the beach huts, we could hear Rover loudly giving tongue under one of them, for he had dug his way under the hut after a rabbit and had filled himself in. There was nothing for it but to dig Rover out. Arthur and I set to and, after about twenty minutes, we got him out. His tongue was hanging out and he was panting furiously. Mrs Robarts then said that we could not play any further because 'Wover' was absolutely exhausted but we would play the four holes home. When we arrived at the clubhouse, Arthur and I were paid for a full round of golf, one shilling and sixpence plus a whole shilling tip for digging Rover out. We thought this was marvellous, to receive half a crown for going round only eight holes. The next couple of times Mr and Mrs Robarts came to play golf we tried the same tactics and they worked like a charm. Rover was a very willing accomplice; the moment he found he was free, he would make for the beach huts as fast as his legs could carry him but, eventaully, I think we were rumbled. Tom King called us one day to say that the Robarts were playing that afternoon and would like us to caddy for them. When they arrived, Rover was wearing a brand new chest harness and Mrs Robarts remarked that there was no way 'Wover' could slip out of that and that the device would save us boys the tiresome task of having to dig him out. All good things must come to an end some time!

A day in the golfing calendar to which we lads always looked forward was the day the Royal West Norfolk members played the annual match against the village golf club. A number of very well known people were members of the Royal West Norfolk Golf Club and often they played in these matches. The Duke of Windsor, when he was Prince of Wales, also Club captain, played in one of them. There were some very good golfers in the village club and they usually won the morning games quite easily. The village club members then went into lunch as guests of the Royal West members and when they came out after lunch the fun really started. I think the parent club members were part of a conspiracy to make the village members slightly inebriated so that they beat them quite easily in the afternoon matches. It was not unknown for one of the village players to take a mighty swish at the ball, miss completely, and fall flat on his face. The caddies would often have to clamber down into some of the deeper bunkers to push and pull a village golfer back on to the fairway.

After the afternoon rounds, everyone excepting us boys retired to the clubhouse. We made our way up the beach road and waited patiently at the bridge to see the next part of the action. Just before the bridge, the road turns fairly sharply to the right whereas, straight ahead, there is a muddy creek, full of water at high tide. About two hours later, the village golfers, their clubs over their shoulders, riding their bicycles, would come rather unsteadily up the beach road, weaving from side to side. Invariably one or two of them failed to negotiate the bend and rode their cycles into the creek, which we thought was hilarious, and, to do them credit, so did some of the victims because, when we helped them out, we often received a few coppers.

The Royal West Norfolk Golf Course runs along a peninsula of land with the North Sea on one side and the saltings on the other. There is an incredible wealth of wildlife. Every spring, three or four pairs of oystercatchers nested on some of the fairways. As the golfers approached, the hen bird ran off the nest, but when the intruder had passed, she returned to continue incubating. On a day when many people were playing, she was

off and on her nest every few minutes, which made it a wonder that her eggs ever hatched, but they usually did. When I go back to play at Brancaster today I look to see if the oystercatchers are nesting where they did when I was a lad; I like to think that some of them are probably descendants of the ones I saw all those years ago.

In the winter time, Brent geese will often feed within a short distance of some of the fairways on the outward holes. Sometimes a thousand or so will be feeding peacefully and, just as you are about to play a shot, they will spring into the air with an outburst of gabbling and fly low over your head and out to sea, passing so low that you feel the down-draught from their wings. As you are playing a quiet round, a marsh harrier might be seen quartering the reeds or even a hen harrier slipping silently round the edges of the dunes. It is difficult to concentrate on your game when there is such a wealth of birdlife all around you. The Army took the golf course as a training ground during the last World War, so that put a stop to my golf for a few years. Some big naval guns were installed on the seaward side of the first fairway and parts of the emplacements are still there to this day, as are the bullet holes in the shelter on the ninth tee, left there by the Army during their training days.

Another exciting time for us boys was when the corn was cut and we were allowed to chase and catch the teeming rabbits which dashed out of the corn as the binder slowly worked its way towards the centre of the field. In those days, most fields were opened by the farm men mowing a swathe round the outsides with scythes; we followed the mowers round the fields, stuffing rolled-up sheets of newspaper down each rabbit hole because we knew that the rabbits that left the corn early would escape to the safety of their holes, but could only go down as far as the newspaper so that, if we arrived quickly, we could put our arms down the holes and pull them out. I wonder how many young keepers of today know that trick. As the binder approached the middle of the field and the rabbits broke cover, we were able to chase and catch them, a jolly good sport which kept us out of mischief and kept us fit. Today, with the speed of the combine harvester, it is not even safe for boys to go into the harvest field.

It may be nostalgia but when I think back, all our summers seemed very long and very hot and our only problem was that there were only twenty-four hours in a day. I often reflect that these harmless activities taught me a great deal of fieldcraft and, at the same time, gave me a love of nature that was to last me the rest of my life.

# 2 · Introduction to Gamekeeping

I left school when I was fourteen and went to work at Sussex Farm: the Second World War was one year old at the time. Had there been no war, I expect I would have followed my father's profession as a fisherman but we were no longer allowed to go out after the whelks as it entailed a long trip out into the North Sea and the risk of being shot at by enemy planes, so most of the fishermen went to work on near-by farms. Unfortunately, I had been at work for only a week when my father died.

The first job I had was crow-scaring, which meant keeping the rooks and jackdaws off two fields of wheat. As fast as I chased them off one field they flew onto the other and when I appeared there they went back to the first. I could see no long term future in chasing backwards and forwards like that. One day I was telling my troubles to my old grandfather and he said, 'You want to trap one of the old sods, boy, and you will never see another crow on that field for a year'. I did as he told me and set three or four traps in the middle of the field, covered them over with a little soil and put some corn on the top of each one. I caught a rook within an hour and, sure enough, I never saw a rook on those fields again whilst I was there.

It is said that the devil makes work for idle hands and I suppose this was true in my case since, no longer having any crows to chase, my thoughts turned towards catching some of the many pheasants which fed on the fields. I coverd the jaws of the trap with strips of sacking and set it in the run along the side of the wire netting on the boundary wood fence. I watched the pheasants come out to feed and when I showed myself they would hurry back to the wood and run up and down the wire netting so that, before long, one was in my trap. I was very careful not to take more than one or two a day and very carefully picked up every feather so that Bill Woodward, the gamekeeper, would not notice anything amiss.

Out in the middle of one of the two fields were two dried pea stacks, put there so that when the peas were threshed the straw that was left could be burned with safety. One day, I noticed several pheasants feeding on the peas that had fallen from the stacks so I hit on the old dodge of soaking some of the peas in a jam jar, putting a pea on a fish hook, tying about a foot of line to the hook and pegging it down. I caught several pheasants like this. One day the farm foreman came to see me and said, 'Angus, you are getting too old  for this job'. (I had only been at it two months.) 'Would you like to go and help Bill Woodward, the gamekeeper? He is looking for a good lad who is interested in wildlife.' It was a bit like asking a duck if he could swim, but I often think that Bill Woodward knew more than I thought. The foreman said he would be sending another young led to see me the next morning; I was to show him how to scare crows and then report to the gamekeeper's house at 9 o'clock. This I did and, as I was about to leave, I said to Peter, the new lad, 'If you want to catch a pheasant, put one of these soaked peas on a fish hook, tie a piece of string on the hook and you will get one'. About ten days after I had been with the gamekeepers, Bill Woodward accused me of teaching young Peter how to catch pheasants. Naturally I denied it, but it appeared that one of the other keepers was walking along the hedgerow, watching his pheasants feeding round the pea stacks when, all of a sudden, one of them flew about thirty feet in the air and then crashed to the ground, flew up and crashed down again. The keeper ran round to the other side of the field, because he had seen the pheasant was flapping nearer and nearer the hedge on that side, and there he saw Peter, with about two hundred and fifty yards of fishing line out and a cock pheasant firmly attached to the other end, gradually hauling him in hand over hand. Unfortunately Peter was given the sack but I was more lucky than I deserved for I got away scot-free to start my gamekeeping career.

When I first started as a keeper's boy, I was a kind of general dogsbody. I had to feed the pheasants in the wood close by the keeper's house but I enjoyed seeing how many came on the feed ride and I still enjoy it to this day. After breakfast I had to exercise the dogs, clean out the kennels and every week do the same for the ferrets. I had to cut kindling wood for the head-keeper's wife, make snare pegs and carry out many similar tasks. One day I was told to box the ratting ferrets: these were a special type of small ferret, not much larger than a stoat and kept just for the ratting. Accompanied by three terrier dogs, who obviously knew more about the job than I did, we went to some corn stacks. The first thing we did was to peg out some wire netting about five yards away from the stacks. The keepers threw the ferrets up onto the thatch of the stack; they quickly disappeared down the rat holes and before long the rats started to leave. Any that ran along the outside we killed with our sticks and any that jumped to the ground were quickly dispatched by the terriers.

Hours later, with many rats accounted for, the ferrets worked their way from the top of the stacks through the holes and runs and eventually came out at the bottom. We picked them up and went home, having done a good job. I thought it was a grand way to earn a living and later I learned how to catch rabbits using ferrets. The ferret is a very hard working and kindly animal if you treat him properly. I have worked them nearly all my life and have not been bitten yet, touch wood! Most of  the hedges in our part of Norfolk were grown on banks which were riddled with rabbit holes. We used a method of netting that I have not seen outside of Norfolk, where most people use purse nets to set, which means walking over the bury and thus alarming the rabbits. We would set a length of net at each side of the bury, about fifteen yards away and straight through a gap at right angles to the hedge, so that the net protruded about ten yards on each side out into the field. Then the ferrets were turned in and we stood by the side of the net, taking rabbits out as fast as they came belting down the hedge. It was not often we had to dig for a laid-up ferret using this method. If we were ferreting in woodland or open buries in the middle of grass fields, we used two long nets set back approximately twenty-five yards, as most rabbits leaving these buries will usually run the same way each time it is ferreted.

The first of April arrived, by which time the pheasants had started to lay. The eggs were collected and stored on corrugated iron sheets tipped at such an angle that, as the bottom eggs were removed, the others gently rolled down thus turning them. Turning eggs daily is very important because, if they are not turned, the yolk of the egg will slowly sink through the white and stick to the shell, making it useless for hatching. In the wild, the hen bird performs this task every time she visits the nest. When sufficient eggs had been collected, they were put under the broody hens to hatch. The broodies were taken off their nests once each day to empty themselves and feed and drink. As each broody was lifted off her nest I had to place a hobble on one leg which I attached to a wooden peg stuck in the ground. This made sure that the right hen was put back on the right nest because sometimes a hen which appeared to be broody did not seem capable of maintaining the correct temperature and her eggs never hatched well, so if she was put back on the wrong nest, she could possibly spoil more than one nest of eggs.

This job was always done at the same time each morning and I learned that it was important to keep to the same time every day because, if you were half an hour late, the broodies became uncomfortable and some would empty themselves in the nests, which then had to be cleaned out; not a nice job! It is a grand place, a big hatching yard with all the old broody hens clucking

away, a sight rarely seen today for most modern keepers use incubators. There are not many old-fashioned chickens nowadays, so broody hens are virtually unobtainable. Years ago, we had to go round the villages every evening, trying to buy broody hens so in some ways I am quite pleased that that side of it is no more. When after twenty-four days the chicks hatched, they and their foster mothers were taken down to the rearing field. The hens were put into coups which faced at every angle so that, if a hawk or any other predator came into the rearing field, the old hens would quickly spot it and give the alarm to the others and the chicks would run to the long grass and hide. There was a keeper on the rearing field all day and sometimes one would take his turn to sleep in the rearing hut at nights.

The rearing field in those days seemed a busy sort of place, with keepers feeding and watering four times a day and moving each coop once, not to mention all the other jobs that needed to be done. It is interesting to reflect how different the feeding was in those days compared with now. Thousands of hens' eggs had to be boiled, shelled and rubbed through a fine sieve; rabbits were cooked and the meat taken from the bones and chopped up very finely before being mixed carefully with the other ingredients and then dried off with biscuit meal so that the food was only just moist. Each batch was mixed just before feed time so that there was no risk of any food becoming stale or sour. Most of the old head keepers had their own special recipes for food and medicine, all closely-guarded secrets because the success of the season, and the keeper's reputation, he felt, depended upon it. Today we empty a sack of specially-prepared concentrated food, delivered from the game-food manufacturer, into a hopper and that lasts the chicks for the rest of the day. With the modern methods, we are able to rear many more pheasants per keeper than we could manage years ago.

One of the more interesting sights on the open rearing field is when the young pheasants are learning to fly. All of a sudden, each poult will take wing at precisely the same time, it is as though someone said, 'Ready, steady, fly', and they all get up together. This usually happens in the early mornings and evenings.

When the pheasant poults were about six weeks old they were moved by horse and cart into the woods. Making sure that every poult was shut up the night before with its foster mother, early next morning at about half past four we slid a wooden bottom under each coop, enabling us to pick up the coop and occupants and place them on the cart for the journey to the wood, where they settled down and enjoyed their new surroundings. They were fed in the woods three times a day.

We had just moved the poults into the wood when all keepering had to stop due to the war and we went to work on the farms to help produce more food. It was about this time that my father's cousin, known as 'Shipmate' (I never ever found out why), asked me if I would like to borrow his old gun. The weapon was a Belgian hammer gun of unknown vintage and I was told, if I held 'her' straight, 'she' would kill at a tremendous distance. The gun had a few dents in the barrels and the stock was held together with screws and some brass wire, but to me if felt like having the use of a Purdey today and it opened up a new life for me. I listened eagerly to Shipmate's stories of wildfowling and shooting. As a young man he had been convicted for poaching but vehemently protested his innocence, insisting in court that the police and gamekeeper who claimed they had found pheasants in his bag were telling lies; his bag was empty because he had hidden the birds in the bushes at Stonecreek!

There is nothing quite like wildfowling, being out on your own under the moon on the great expanse of marsh with the roar of the sea, the voices of the geese, the whistling of the wigeon and the cry of the curlew in your ears. I seldom shot more than one or two birds a night and many was the time I returned empty-handed. The great thrill was working out where the duck ought to be feeding, going and finding the preening feathers which told you they had visited that spot the night before and waiting with great expectations of a full bag, only to find that the fowl had decided to go somewhere else. I

always convinced myself I would get it right the next time.

Whenever I am down the harbour, I remember the exact spot where I shot my first goose. I can still see that massive skein coming towards me as, all those years ago, I hid behind one of the whelk boats. I took careful aim at the leading gander, pulled the trigger and, to my amazement, the third and fourth birds of the skein fell out of the sky, both killed with the same shot.

Those early years of my shooting life were mostly spent wildfowling, in the company of my faithful flatcoat retriever named Judy. She was the first dog I ever owned and was eighteen months old when she was given to me by a Belgian Pilot Officer, stationed at Bircham Newton airfield but who lived at Brancaster Staithe; he was moving overseas and could not take her with him. Judy was a clever bitch and as I had virtually no knowledge of how to train a dog we both learned together. Her knowledge of the marshes was even greater than my own and if, for any reason, we lost one another at night flight, I would find her waiting at the back door on my return home. One thing Judy taught herself was, when I was creeping, on hands and knees up to some duck feeding or sheltering in a creek or drain, to be at my heels also slinking along on her belly. On one occasion I had been very lucky on my way down to the sea wall, for Judy had flushed two partridges and a pheasant, all of which I shot. I then went out onto the saltings for evening flight. When I was on my way home in the dark, I decided that I would not take the partridge and pheasant home with me just in case I met the local bobby. I had shot the birds where I had full rights, but I did not have a game licence, being unable to afford the £3. All I had was a ten-shilling gun licence which entitled me to shoot only rabbits, pigeon and wildfowl. I followed Shipmate's example and hid the birds in the sea blite bushes at Stonecreek for collection later that night.

After I had eaten my supper, I went with Judy to collect the birds, which were hidden about half a mile from our house. We were within three hundred yards of the spot when Judy went off ahead of me, which was most unusual for she always stayed at heel unless I had sent her out to hunt or retrieve. I stood and listened and could hear her splashing through the mud and water near the bushes and, a short time later, I heard her coming back and knew by her snuffling pant that she was carrying something; sure enough, she brought me the pheasant. I then told her to 'Go fetch', and off she went and made two more trips, bringing the brace of partridges, one at a time. It amazed me that she had remembered exactly where the game was hidden.

A day or two later, I hid a duck in the same spot and went home in a different direction from normal; later that night I walked with Judy to the bottom of our garden where it joined

the saltings and sent her to 'Fetch'. Shortly after she came back with the duck and, from that day, if I had shot any game I hid it in the same place, going with her as far as the back door until I judged it was safe to collect whatever had been left, and she never failed to bring home the bacon. If we had been lucky and shot more than one, I tied the legs and necks together so that she had to make only one trip. If ever a dog was born to please her master it was she, asking me only for a place by the fire, a full belly and to be allowed to accompany me wherever I went. Ever since those early days with Judy I have been a strong believer in telepathy between man and dog; many times I have been concentrating on what I wanted my dog to do and it has anticipated my thoughts by turning at the right time or going to the very spot I had in mind.

We finished work at four o'clock in the afternoon and it usually took me five or six minutes to get home but, when the duck-shooting season was on, I used to fly home as hard as I could pedal my bike and rush through the front door to where my mother had a cup of tea poured and a sandwich ready. I would drink the tea, grab my gun and bag, and Judy and I would go out of the back door and onto the marsh, just in time to catch the evening flight, with me eating the sandwiches as I went. Judy was always waiting for me, sitting on the pavement at the top of our yard looking down the road in the direction she knew I would be coming from. Mother said Judy would be sleeping on the mat in front of the fire and, at four o'clock promptly, she would get up, stretch herself and ask to be let out and would go straight to the top of the yard and wait fo me to come home. Mother said that Judy was so regular in her timekeeping that she did not have to look at the clock to know that it was four o'clock.

When I joined the Army, she still waited for me to come home every night for about three weeks, but then she finally gave up and did not bother any more to go to the gate and wait. Eventually I was posted to the Middle East and, after I had been out there for nearly a year, I received news of my release from service. A month later I was back in England but we were not allowed to write home disclosing our whereabouts, only send a telegram saying 'Arrived in England'. Three weeks later I was finally discharged. I did not get my discharge papers until eight o'clock in the morning and by nine o'clock was on my way home, having been unable to let my mother know I was coming. I arrived home at twenty minutes past two on the Eastern Counties bus; the bus stop was about one hundred and fifty yards from our house and, as I stood on the step waiting for it to slow down, I could see Judy waiting on the pavement by our gate. I had barely stepped off the bus when she came galloping up the road to greet me and what a welcome I received. My mother told me later that she knew I was coming home that afternoon because Judy went to her usual place at two o'clock and refused to come back into the house. How did that dog know I was on my way back? I expect that, as I was riding home, my thoughts were of once more being able to do all the things I loved and I included her in my thoughts.

Judy lived until she was fourteen and we enjoyed a great many happy days roaming the saltings and marshes together. She moved house with me when I married and moved to Holme-Next-Sea. She thought the world of our two children and made a point of lying near their pram and growling at any stranger who came a bit too close. She enjoyed rolling on the floor and playing with them, playfully taking a hand or foot into her mouth as though she was going to bite, but of course she never did. Although she enjoyed the children, I suspect she thought that wildfowling was much more fun.

I changed jobs from Sussex Farm to Field House Farm, still working for the same employer. I was asked to look after two riding horses, hand-milk a couple of cows that produced milk for the manager's house and a few farmworkers' cottages and rear a litter of young pigs. This job was a change from what I had been used to and it took me all one Saturday afternoon to learn to milk the two cows, one of which was virtually dry and gave only about two pints of milk. Whatever those patient animals must have felt about my ham-fisted attempts to milk them I hate to think. I had been doing this job for about a month when, one Tuesday morning, the manager told me that he was going to King's Lynn to buy another cow for me because there was not enough milk to supply the house and the farmworkers. Later that afternoon, a cattle lorry arrived containing a pretty Jersey cow which I was told needed milking immediately. The lorry driver helped me get her into the cow shed, I gave her some food and she started eating straight away, behaving as quietly as a lamb. I fetched the milk pail and stool, sat myself down with the pail between my knees and moved her leg back so I could milk her; she took no notice whatsoever, but as soon as I touched her teat she lashed out with her hind leg, knocking me off the stool, clean as a whistle. I landed just outside the cow-shed door. With those lovely, sad eyes that all Jersey cows seem to have, she looked round at me lying there and then kicked the pail out the door as well! When I told the manager what had happened, he said, 'Didn't anyone tell you she is a heifer that has only been calved two days and never been milked by hand?' I would not have been surprised, knowing his sense of humour, that he had purposely forgot to tell me!

When I came into work one morning, I went as usual to feed the litter of pigs and, as I did so, I counted them and found I was one short. I knew it was impossible for one to have jumped out of the sty and, even if he had found a way out, he would not have been able to escape from the main building because the door was shut and locked. I reported the loss to the manager who mumbled something about 're-arranging' the pigs, which to me was a mystery. A couple of days later the problem was solved when I was given a nice joint of pork to take home and told to keep my mouth shut. A lot of pigs went the way of that one during the war.

About a year later, a group of Land Army girls moved into some of the vacant cottages on the farm; they worked in the place of men who had either joined the forces as volunteers or been called up. I had to teach one of these girls to do my work so that I could move back onto the farm. What fun and games we had, for the Land Army girls got into all kinds of muddles trying to put harness on the cart-horses which towered above them. It was quite a common sight to see a runaway horse heading back to the stables as fast as his legs could carry him with a very frightened girl's face peering out of the cart. When

we started threshing the corn stacks, four or five girls worked, pitching sheaves onto the drum until one of them picked up a sheaf which held a rat or a mouse. There would be a chorus of squeals and the rats and mice very soon had the stack yard to themselves. They worked jolly hard, those girls, doing some really back-breaking jobs like carrying sacks of potatoes, knocking and topping sugar beet and loading dung carts, but they were always cheerful. It was very interesting to see that, after the girls had been there a few weeks, even the older men who normally came to work with patches or holes in their clothes began to appear more smartly dressed. Perhaps it was just as well that after shave lotion was not used often by the men in those days or who knows what heavenly smells the horses would have had to endure.

One of the men who worked on the farm was nick-named Gobbler; he was as strong as a horse and was very proud of it, always showing off his feats of strength, but unfortunately he had little brain power. One day he came into the yard with a horse and cart and tried to get the horse to back the cart under the hovel into the dry. This particular horse had injured its back several years before and, although it was a tremendous horse at pulling, it could not, or would not, go backwards. After several attempts to back horse and cart into the shed, Gobbler took the horse out of the shafts and tied him up to a post. Then he picked up the shafts himself, pushed the cart into the shed and, turning to the horse, said, 'There, I hope you feel bloody well ashamed of yourself'.

I spent a lot of time at weekends sailing. The owners of the boats, mostly twelve-metre Sharpies, were nearly always short of a crew, especially if there was a stiff breeze and a bit of extra ballast was needed. Sailing is a grand sport with the sound of the wind and the water and the feel of the boat underneath straining to go faster. I often crewed for a Major Whittaker who had lost a leg in the 1914–1918 war. He had a small trolley fitted in the boat on which he sat and swivelled round the stern every time we went about. He never sailed with his artificial leg on in case we turned over. One of the locals, Barney Pells, looked after the Major's boat and, one day, when we came ashore after having lost another race, the Major was rather displeased, to say the least. Barney came down the road swinging the artificial leg over his shoulder; we strapped it on and left the Major standing in about two feet of water. When we had taken the sails down, Barney picked up the main sail and boom and, as he turned round, the end of it hit the artificial leg, dumping the Major on his backside in water which just about came up to his chin. Oh, didn't he swear! The funny part was that, every now and again, a  small wave would cover his mouth and drown his vocabulary but he made up for it as soon as his mouth was out of the water.

Another lovely character was Mrs Lesley, wife of Colonel

Jack, known affectionately to everyone as Margot. She was nearly always accompanied by a half a dozen dogs and quite often she lost one or two of them. Then she drove round the village, calling them with the car horn, so that if any car came down the High Street and sounded its hooter too insistently, one of the locals in the pub would look up from his game of dominoes and say, 'Sounds as if Margot has lost one of her dogs again'. Mrs Lesley was very careful over her health and read somewhere that a good way to avoid colds was to gargle every night with sea water. She asked my brother if he would take some bottles out to sea with him and fill them with salt water when he was a long way out to avoid any pollution. This worked well for many months until, one day, brother forgot to take the bottles and Mrs Lesley called the very next day for them. My mother kept her talking while brother and I nipped out of the back door and down to the creek. Fortunately the tide was in and we quickly strained some salt water through some muslin and filled the bottles and off she went quite happily. We filled her bottles from the creek for many more years and one night, when mother was waiting at table at Apple Tree Cottage, she overheard Mrs Lesley telling her guests what a good thing for the throat gargling with salt water was and also insisting that the water must, like her own supply, be obtained from miles out to sea.

It is interesting to compare work on the farm then and now. Years ago, the farmworker took great pride in his work. He had to, I suppose, because if he did anything shoddy, like building a stack that needed a pole to hold it up, or ploughing a crooked furrow, he had his leg pulled mercilessly for weeks afterwards. Some of the work was very hard for the men, let alone us boys who were expected to lift and carry sacks of corn and fertiliser alongside the men. The combines were just starting to appear at that time and at Sussex and Field House Farms we had two of them. Some of the early combines dropped sacks of corn on the ground all over the field and these, weighing between fourteen and eighteen stones each, had to be lifted up into a horse-drawn wagon and taken back to the farms and tipped into the barn. This entailed walking up a long plank with a sack of corn across your shoulders and tipping it on top of a large heap. At one harvest, when I was sixteen years of age, I did this from seven o'clock in the morning until nine o'clock at night and went home with my shoulders red raw from the chafe of the rough corn sacks. There was not so much corn grown in those days as now, so thankfully that back-breaking job did not last long.

The majority of the ploughing on the farm was done with tractors but we still worked some fields with horses, a most enjoyable job. There are not many people still working on the farms who have had the pleasure of ploughing with horses. Instead of the roar of the tractor, there was just the occasional gentle cough of one of the horses, the sound of the soil coming off the plough-share, the jingle of the harness and the constant cry of the seagulls which competed for the worms that were turned up out of the ground. I loved working with horses; they are such noble animals, not asking much out of life, just a warm

stable, some good food and a bit of kindness and they repay you by working for you eight hours a day.

Some of the corn was taken in sacks to the railway at Burnham Market and went away by train. The horses would receive an extra grooming until their coats shone like silk; their manes and tails were plaited with coloured ribbons and a special road harness with lots of highly-polished brass attached to it was taken out of the harness room and put on their backs. I am sure the horses knew when they were going on an outing because even the most sedate one would start prancing and showing off for, like us, they enjoyed a change from the normal routine.

Mr Henry Thompson, who owned Sussex Farm, grew a lot of potatoes, mostly Majestic and Arran Banner, which produced a white flower. One year, Mr Thompson imported from Ireland some special seed which grew purple flowers. One day, as he was driving through the farm past the farmworkers' cottages, he noticed that all the gardens had potatoes with purple flowers and, turning to his farm manager, he said, 'It is marvellous how every year I seem to grow the same variety of potato as my men!'

I had to join the Home Guard when I was about sixteen. I was made what was called Officer's Runner (I never did find out just what it meant) and given a sten gun and eighty-five rounds of ammunition. This was heaven for someone who loved guns as much as I did; the only trouble was I never 'officially' fired it, although I was able to get plenty of spare rounds from one of the regular soldiers stationed on the common, guarding one of the early types of radar stations. With a friend, I went out on the marshes and shot at rabbits on the 'knod', which was a small group of sand dunes infested by rabbits. These conies left their holes in the dunes to feed on the marshes; we would creep up quietly and get between them and their buries and shoot at them as they dashed back. Whilst I was in the Home Guard, some soldiers from the Scots Guards came to teach us how to find our way about at night and, in particular, how to find our way through the Downs woods. This seemed very strange to Bill Peacher and myself because the pair of us spent several nights a year poaching in these woods and knew every tree.

Whilst some of the older men in the village were keen on training and square-bashing, most of us younger ones had other things on our minds. The night the enemy bombed Coventry, they laid a flare path of incendiary bombs from the coast for the rest of the planes to follow to the target. I had just come home from a dance when I heard all the commotion and went out to see what was happening. It was the job of the ARP (the Air Raid Patrol) to deal with this kind of emergency; they were better trained than the Home Guard, or so they kept telling us. The ARP trained in groups of three, one man had a stirrup pump, one a bucket of water and the third a bucket of sand. They practised for many hours, putting out imaginary incendiary bombs, but, when it came to the real thing, they discovered that the man with the pump lived at one end of the village, the man with the bucket lived at the other (nearly a mile away), while the man with the sand bucket lived somewhere in between! By the time they all found one another in the dark, most of the incendiaries had burned themselves out.

When I was eighteen I joined the Army. I was very fortunate because, when I had completed my training and was on embarkation leave, the war with Germany came to an end and, not long afterwards, the Japanese surrendered. I saw service in Egypt and Palestine and was in Palestine when my discharge from the Army came through. Men who had worked on the farms before the War were released early to help with the production of food which was so much needed, both during and after the war.

Shortly after my release, I married and went to work as a cowman for a Mr Will Renault at Holme-Next-Sea. We milked by hand about forty cows, night and morning, but after a few months we had a milking machine which made our life much easier. After I had had a couple of narrow squeaks with the

Ayrshire bull, the boss decided for safety's sake, and before someone was killed, to get rid of the bull and use artificial insemination. This was another improvement because it gave the dairy farmer the chance to use a top-class sire without the cost of buying one and, as anyone knows who has worked with bulls, they are dangerous beasts. It was noticeable that, after a few years, our milk yield went up considerably when the offspring of the better breeding came into the milking herd.

I worked for five years at Holme and, during any spare time I had in the winter, spent many a happy hour rabbiting, which made me start thinking about once more becoming a gamekeeper. Although I thoroughly enjoyed most aspects of the farm work, my true love was for wildlife and nature. After spending many hours talking this over with my wife Audrey, she said that, if keepering was the job I really wanted to do, she would be quite happy to move. This was a very big decision for her to leave her family and friends and move to a strange part of the country where she knew no one. It was not so difficult for me because I would be doing the job I loved and, like an old cock pheasant, just coming home to feed and roost. Shortly after I saw an advertisement in the local paper for an under-keeper's job at Rothwell. I obtained references from my employer, wrote for the situation and was invited to go for an interview at which I was offered the job at £6 per week with a house. I still have my letter of appointment. I eagerly accepted and went back home to work out a fortnight's notice before starting out on my new life.

# 3 · Rothwell

We arrived at Rothwell, my wife Audrey, our two small children, Rodney and Angela, plus a budgerigar travelling in the back of a furniture van. It must have been a great ordeal for my wife because she had not seen the house before we arrived but she quickly settled in. Rothwell Estate was a famous partridge manor in those days, owned by Mr Joseph Nickerson. Later he was knighted and Sir Joseph, farmer and seedsman, is a brilliant shot and one of the most knowledgeable men in the country on partridges. In another world, he would have made a very good head keeper. I learned more about partridges at Rothwell in five years than most gamekeepers have the opportunity to learn in a lifetime.

The head keeper was Bill Jacobs, a very hard man to work for but always fair, one of the old school who kept all of us on our toes. There were five of us under keepers at that time. Jimmy Needs was my next-door beat keeper and it was from him that I gained much of my knowledge of partridges. He was also a brilliant man with a trap, something that I took to like a duck to water. It has always been my proud boast that I can catch any of the predators that we have to deal with. (I much prefer the word predator to vermin; why call a bird or animal vermin just because it is doing what is instinctive to it in order to live?) Jimmy Needs was not only a very good gamekeeper, but he

49

also had that wonderful ability to teach and was always ready to pass on his knowledge. It was tragic that he died while still a comparatively young man.

I am sorry to say that many of the young keepers of today are more interested in the gun than the trap. While the gun is, and always will be, a very important tool of our trade, the trap is one hundred times as efficient. A series of correctly-set traps is on duty for twenty-four hours a day all over the estate, but there is only one gun working where the keeper happens to be at the time. The number of stoats and weasels one shoots in a year comes a very poor second to the numbers that can be trapped. I had about a hundred and fifty traps working on my beat at Rothwell, mostly set in tunnels but also a few isolated ones in odd rabbit holes. These ones often caught stoats, weasels or rats that missed the main tunnel traps. The best site for a tunnel trap, I found, was to dig it into the bank, crossways through the hedge (so that whichever side of the hedge a stoat or weasel runs he must come across the tunnel) and about twenty-five yards short of the hedge end. I found this out one day quite by accident when I had gone out without a gun and

spotted a stoat thoroughly working in a hedge ahead of me until he was about twenty yards from the end, at which point he cut across the corner of the field, missing the two tunnels set on each hedge end. After this observation, I moved my tunnels back up the hedge and found they worked more efficiently. It is very important, every three or four days, to spring and reset any traps that have not caught anything, otherwise they might not spring when something light like a weasel passes over them. It is also important to keep the soil at each end freshly turned because most animals are attracted by fresh earth. I always carried a worn-out carrot hoe for this purpose; it only took a few seconds on each daily visit to disturb the soil. I am not suggesting that every keeper should have hundred and fifty tunnels operating, for I was a partridge keeper and had only a thousand acres to look after, whereas many keepers today have anything up to three thousand acres and have to rear pheasants as well. A few traps in the right places are a useful aid to the busiest keeper.

As I was walking from one tunnel to the next, I would be looking for signs of perhaps a bitch stoat having born a litter of young in an old rabbit bury or somewhere like that. The telltale signs are the remains of old food, such as a partly-eaten rabbit, wing of a song bird or where the stoats have made lots of runs through the grass. If I found a litter of stoats, I would try and squeak out the old bitch first and shoot her. If this was not successful, I would then set traps in every hole and also on some of the runs. It was always a great relief to get the bitch because then the young ones were quite easy to deal with. If she got away, she would very quickly move her young and cause tremendous damage among the nests of partridge and song brids before being finally accounted for, and very often you do not get a second chance. When a litter of stoats is born in a particular spot, they systematically work a large area; nothing is safe, neither game nor song birds. I have even seen stoats thirty feet up a tree after a pigeon's nest. I once saw a bitch stoat in a blackbird's nest bite through the wings of the young birds so

they were unable to get away and toss them over the side of the nest onto the ground, where the young stoats were waiting to kill each one as it fell. This was a unique opportunity for me to watch and learn, because this nest was in a hawthorn bush in the middle of a meadow and I knew I could shoot the stoats any time I wanted, without the fear of their getting away.

When the 1st May came round, Jimmy Needs and I started partridge-nesting, walking down every hedge, one each side, looking in the grass, marking each nest with a hazel stick. In a book, we recorded the date found, how many eggs and other useful information. We tried to visit each nest every day or so and recorded, in our books, the progress of each nest until it had either hatched or been destroyed by a predator or the weather. It was essential to write all this down, as no-one can keep an accurate account in his head of what is happening to as many as a hundred nests. When the information from the books of every keeper on the estate was recorded on the large map, it gave a very interesting picture of what had happened that season. One could see where a litter of stoats had cleaned out all the nests round two fields before it had been dealt with, that a badger, on a particular night, had travelled across the estate up and down different hedgerows or a fox, living over the boundary, was making raids on some particular hedges. Sometimes it was hedgehogs causing problems.

I should mention the fact that a good keeper must be able to look at any nest which has been destroyed and say exactly which predator was responsible; different predators have their own distinctive methods of dealing with a nest. For instance, a badger does not often kill the sitting bird but he minces up the eggs extremely thoroughly in his mouth and puts the very finely chewed shell back in the nest. A hedgehog is similar, but he does not chew the eggs into such small pieces and usually strews the remains around the outside of the nest. A fox nearly always kills the sitting bird and eats the eggs, shells and all, although sometimes he will leave two or three eggs and at other times will not eat any of them. I think it depends on how hungry he is or, if it is a vixen with cubs, she will eat the eggs and go back to the earth, carrying the sitting partridge or pheasant, and regurgitate the eggs for her cubs. A stoat sometimes kills and sometimes does not kill the sitting bird. The first clue is when you find an egg hidden a short way from the nest. If you hunt around you can find most of the eggs hidden in small groups and partially covered up. Sometimes they are buried in mole runs.

I remember going out on my rounds very early one morning just after daybreak; I checked a partridge and a pheasant sitting within about ten yards of each other who both had only two days to go before hatching. I happened to come back that way about two hours later when, to my surprise, I saw that both hens were off the nest and all the eggs had gone. I soon realised that a stoat was the culprit and, as I thought that neither of the birds had been killed, I decided that, as the eggs were due to hatch in a couple of days, there was a good chance that, if I could replace them, the parent birds might return. I hunted up and down the hedge and eventually found all but two of the pheasant eggs which I returned to her nest, but I could find no partridge eggs. I was about to give up when, under a feeding shelter, I saw a stoat pop his head out of a mole run. I squeaked a couple of times and, when he popped his head out again, I shot him. Then I dug out some of the mole runs very carefully with my hands and recovered all the eighteen partridge eggs. These I placed back in her nest and went home for breakfast. I came back again at lunchtime and, to my great pleasure, I saw that both birds were back on their nests. A couple of days later, both clutches hatched successfully.

When a carrion crow takes a nest of eggs, he nearly always eats them a few yards away from the nest but a magpie will often carry the eggs to a favourite tree or bush and eat them there; a magpie will also tear the lining out of the nest. I once saw a bush that magpies had been using and there were over a hundred egg shells at the foot of it. This I hasten to add was not on my estate!

When we found a nest, we would first of all deepen the scrape because, when a scrape is not deep enough, and the hen partridge is ready to incubate, she may make it too flat and some of the eggs will roll out when she moves about, goes off to feed or turns the eggs. We made a hole about four inches

deep in the bottom of the scrape, plugged it with some sheep's wool and poured a little Renardine on it. We covered this with a thin layer of soil, for Renardine is a very evil-smelling liquid made especially for keeping moles and foxes away from the nest. Moles will often tunnel up through the bottom of the nest in their search for food and the eggs will roll down the mole run. Moles leave the fields during dry spells and work in the hedges and woodlands where the ground is moist due to the shade of the bushes and trees. There they can find their food much more easily for, during dry spells, worms go down very deep. It is very noticeable that, as soon as it starts to rain after a dry spell, the mole is very quickly back working the fields.

Sometimes a partridge will decide to nest in a place where there is hardly any vegetation. In such a case, we waited until she had laid three eggs, then cut a few small twigs from the hedge, stuck them in the ground leaning them over the nest and returned every day to add a few more. This had to be done very gradually over four or five days because, if too much cover is placed over the nest too quickly, the partridge might desert. The reason for 'bushing-up' the nest is to try to hide it from the sharp eyes of the rooks, carrion crows and other winged predators.

I often think that the predatory birds and animals have far more brains and skills at their command than we human beings give them credit for. An example of this was at Rothwell, where Sir Joseph had the sporting rights over a large sheep farm. The sheep would eat all the vegetation right up to the hedge and leave the partridge sitting in the open where the nests could be seen very easily and it was not long before the rooks and jackdaws found them and stole the eggs. To try to avoid this problem, I knocked stakes into the ground, one on each side of the nest next to the hedge and about two yards away from it and another in front of the nest. I fixed a short piece of

sheep netting around the stakes, making a half-diamond minia-
ture pen. I did about ten nests as an experiment and every one
hatched successfully. The next year I fenced every nest that
I found in the sheep fields, about twenty-five in all. They
hatched very well but I lost seven or eight to foxes. The
following year I again fenced every nest I found in those fields
and never had a single one hatch; the foxes took the lot. I am
sure they had learned that, in all those small pens of lush
vegetation, they would find a sitting partridge.

Another instance concerned winged predators. A very good
keeper friend looked after a large shoot on Salisbury Plain.
Running through the estate were some wide roadways, along
which the Army used to drive tanks. These roads were
separated from the arable fields by barbed-wire fences and it
was by those fences that the partridge and pheasants made their
nests. The keeper was single-handed so he rallied his family and
any other help he could muster to help him find the nests. When
they found a nest, it was marked by tying a piece of binder
string on the wire fence. The keeper was thus able to save a lot
of time and cover much more ground by driving his Landrover
from nest to nest. This worked well for the first couple of years
but then rooks and jackdaws discovered that by every piece of
string there was a nest. They robbed many nests before the
keeper one day actually saw a rook fly along the wire fence, find
a piece of string, land and walk straight to the nest. When he
removed all the string and marked the nests in a subtler way,
the losses ceased immediately. Nature is far more clever than
we realise.

The English or grey partridge pairs for life but if one is killed
the other will take another mate. It is lovely to watch them
pairing on a nice spring-like day in late January or February. If
the old birds of the covey have survived the winter, they are
usually the first ones to start pairing. They chase one another
backwards and forwards over twenty-yard stretch, both turning exactly at the same moment and talking to each other all the
time. If you take the trouble to go and look where they have

been 'jugging' or sleeping in the field at night, you will notice that, whereas before they started pairing their droppings were close together, because the covey had huddled together to keep warm, their droppings will show that they are now sleeping in twos, each pair just a little way apart from the others. Gradually, they move further and further apart until at last they take up their own particular piece of hedgerow where they will eventually nest. The cook partridge can be very pugnacious, particularly if he is an old bird and will claim a much larger territory than a young·one. This is a very good reason why a young stock is always the best, plus the fact that a young hen will usually lay more eggs, up to sixteen or eighteen, compared to, say, twelve for an old hen.

The grey partridge usually makes anything from one to three scrapes in the hedge bottom and eventually selects one where she will lay her eggs. If the hen is an old bird, she will cover her eggs with pieces of dead grass right from the start but a young hen may not cover them until she has laid perhaps three eggs. The hen will not lay every day but will miss one or two during the laying period. She always removes the dead grass when she comes to the nest and carefully replaces it when she leaves, adding a little more on each visit. When the hen is reaching the end of her clutch of eggs, she will gradually work all the dead grass covering her eggs underneath them to make a lovely nest.

She will also polish each egg between her wings and body until it shines like a full moon. Then she arranges the eggs around the nest most beautifully, we call it laid-out ready for sitting, and then leaves the nest, not to return for twenty-four hours whilst she feeds and feeds. She will then return and begin incubation.

When the hen starts to sit you have to be especially careful during the first eight or nine days as to how you approach the nest. If she is frightened off during the first week, she will very often desert and all your time and effort will be wasted and you will have lost a covey of young partridges because there is the strong possibility she may not nest again. If she does nest again she will lay only seven, eight or nine eggs and, if it happens to be a cold, wet autumn, there will be little chance of her rearing any young at all. During the twenty-four-day incubation period when the hen is sitting, her mate faithfully remains on station out in the field about one hundred yards away from the nest. He is ever watchful for danger and will warn his mate if anything threatens; he stands guard over her while she feeds and escorts her back to the nest when she is ready to return. When the eggs are ready to hatch, the cock and hen may be heard talking to one another quite loudly. After a while, the cock will come to the side of the hen and make a very shallow scrape close by the nest and, as the chicks hatch, the hen will pass some of them to him to brood and to dry off. I have sometimes climbed a tree and watched them and it is a lovely thing to see. As soon as the chicks are thoroughly dried, the parent birds will take them away from the nest into a field of corn or other such cover and share the rearing of the brood.

I have said how shy the English partridge is during her first week of incubation, but there was a sweet old lady living in a cottage on part of my beat at Rothwell who used to feed the farm cats for a Mr Strawson. One day she said to me, 'Keeper, I see you are spending a lot of time looking for nests. If I told you where there was one would you take the eggs?' I assured her that the reason we looked for nests was because we only wished to protect them and we always left the eggs for the partridge to hatch. She said, 'I know where there is a nest and the eggs keep rolling out and I don't know what to do, otherwise I would not have told you'. We went into the farmyard where the partridges had made a nest in a straw stack and, as the hen had made up her nest, so the eggs had rolled out. I made the nest much deeper and put the eggs back and a couple of days later the hen strated to sit.

When I spoke to the old lady a few days later, she was so pleased that she offered to show me her pet partridge. She took me out to her garden, walked up the path to the bank at the end and said, 'Here is my pet'. To my amazement, she bent down and stroked the hen partridge on the nest and when I looked more closely there was a Shippam's Potted Meat jar on each side of the nest, one containing corn, the other water. If I had not seen her actually stroke the partridge I do not think I would have believed it.

That season was one of the worst I can remember. A cold windy rain began late on a Wednesday night and continued until the Sunday with hardly a break. It was heartbreaking going round my nests, as nearly every hen had been forced to give up sitting due to the cold and wet. It takes a good deal to make an English partridge desert her nest after she has been sitting a fortnight. On the Sunday morning, I was passing my old lady's house and I called in to check the nest in her garden. I walked up the path with my coat collar well pulled up to try and  keep out the driving rain, feeling thoroughly dejected as most of the birds I had visited that morning had deserted. As I reached the end of the path, I looked up and, to my amazement, saw a large black umbrella open with the handle stuck in the bank and the old lady's pet bird sitting underneath, dry as a bone. She was one of the very few partridges to rear a covey that year.

Sometimes, for reasons best known to itself, a partridge will choose to nest in a place where there is a very good chance that she will be disturbed by farm cats, dogs or cattle passing through the gateway. When we found such a nest, we waited until she had laid six eggs, took them and gave her some wooden or dummy ones that looked exactly like her own. We visited the nest every day, taking her eggs as she laid them and adding more dummy ones, and eventually she began to incubate them. The real eggs, and others that had been collected in this way over the whole of the estate, were then placed under bantams, a batch being set every two days. After the partridge had been sitting for twelve or fourteen days, we would gently ease her off the nest with a long stick, take her dummy eggs and place fifteen chipped ones in their place. This method (called the Euston System as it was first used on the Duke of Grafton's Euston Estate in Suffolk) cut down the danger period by several days and if, by any chance, she was disturbed, instead of losing both bird and eggs, the eggs could be distributed among other nests.

It is a great tragedy that the English or grey partridge has declined so much over the last twenty-five years. Modern farming and spraying of crops are generally blamed for this, but I feel another important factor is the ever-rising cost of shooting. There are far fewer private shoots nowadays, mostly syndicates, and those that are still private are often obliged to sell days' shooting to offset the costs; the safest way of seeing a return for your money is to concentrate on the pheasants. You cannot expect a syndicate member to pay for a season's shooting only to be told he cannot shoot that year because the partridges have not been able to rear any young due to the wet summer. There are far fewer keepers than there were years ago, most of them trying to look after far too big an acreage to do the job properly and, with the modern concentration on pheasants, not many young keepers are having the training that those of my age group received.

Partridge-keepering is a specialised job and it can be rewarding but also very frustrating. When you have walked hundreds of miles around tunnel traps and searched for nests, visited them often and done all you possibly can to help, then to see your work ruined by bad weather teaches you great patience and you console yourself with the thought that next season must be better. Although the partridge season is open from September to the end of January at Rothwell, we shot partridges only during the month of October: this is how most estates carried on in those days, the rest of the season been taken up with pheasant shooting.

I was once out with Sir Joseph on another estate where most of the beaters were old-age pensioners. As one of the drives was drawing to its close, a large covey of English partridge swung down the line of guns, breaking back over the beaters' heads. As the boss put his gun up, one of the old beaters dropped onto his knees in the sugar beet. Sir Joseph called to him saying, 'You're quite safe, my man; I've never shot a beater in my life'. As the old man climbed stiffly to his feet, he replied, 'No, governor; and I don't intend being the first bugger'.

Of the two things I shall always remember about the grey

partridge, one is being out at dusk on a winter's night and listening to them calling to one another as they prepare to jug in the middle of a ploughed field. The other is, on a lovely autumn day during the shooting season, standing back from a very high thorn hedge and hearing a covey talking to one another as they fly towards you and, as they top the hedge, exploding in all directions, usually so quickly that you cannot let your gun off.

As soon as we had finished the partridge-shooting season, Jimmy Needs and I teamed up to go rabbiting. There were thousands on the estate before the coming of that awful disease, myxomatosis. We ran twelve dozen traps and not only did we catch large numbers of rabbits, but we also caught a lot of rats and stoats. When we had finished seeing to our traps each morning about breakfast time, we spent the rest of the day ferreting. Rabbits did not bolt very well at Rothwell, so we spent most of our time digging them out with a line ferret.

A line ferret is a large male ferret, known as a 'buck' or 'hob' in different counties. He has a soft leather collar around his neck to which is attached a fairly stout cord about fifteen yards long which we call a ferret line – hence the term 'line ferret'. The line has a mark in it one yard from the collar and from there it is marked at two-yard intervals so, at any time when we are digging, we know how far we are from the ferret. When the line goes tight that means that the ferret has killed and we then follow the line by digging holes every yard or so along the line, or 'springing', until we come to the ferret and rabbit.

Digging was hard work, but it was also good sport. We only ferreted the more shallow buries and trapped the deeper places. Jimmy owned two wonderful terriers, Tinker and Patch, who saved us hours and hours of digging by pin-pointing where the rabbits and ferrets were in the bury so that, instead of digging perhaps four or five holes and following the line, we were able to dig straight down to where the ferret killed.

Tinker had been caught in traps a couple of times and, from then on, he seemed to develop a sixth sense for one and kept well away. Many was the time I saw him in full cry after a

rabbit which was heading for a bank
where there was a line of traps and, if
Tinker could not catch the rabbit, he
would stop short of the traps and
come back to us. One might say it
was because he had seen us set the
traps, but in several incidents either he
had not been present at the time they
were set or the traps belonged to a
neighbouring keeper working a boun-
dary hedge, and there was no way he could possibly have
known about them except by instinct. He was a remarkable
dog. When we arrived at our traps first thing in the morning,
we put our ferret boxes down in a sheltered spot and Tinker
would lie beside them and go to sleep waiting patiently until we
returned. This may not have been until mid-day, but he was
always there when we came back. We believed he would stay
with our ferret boxes for days, even if we did not come back to
them. He was a wonderful working mate and it is such a shame
that dogs have such short lives.

We do not seem to get the plagues of starlings nowadays like
we did thirty years ago. They used to congregate on the field
just beside Fox Cover Wood, so thickly that a stone could not
be thrown onto the field without hitting one. They would take
off with a roar like thunder and settle in the woods to roost.
There was an eighteen-inch layer of droppings in the woods and
the sheer weight of their numbers broke the branches from the
trees. We tried all the things we could think of, guns, bonfires
and fireworks, but nothing would shift them and eventually
they killed the whole wood before they decided to move
elsewhere. The starling is about the only bird that I do not like
and I am sorry to say that I cannot find a good word to say
about him.

When Sir Joseph heard that I had spent much of my youth
wildfowling, he asked me if I would like to accompany him
when he went duck-shooting on Read's Island in the Humber

estuary. Read's Island is a wildfowler's dream, a wild and lonely place, the only disturbance to the wild cries of the ducks, waders and geese was the occasional barge that chugged up or down the river. We would leave our transport in a farmer's yard and were met at the jetty by Jock Campbell, who ferried us out to the island in an ex-WD landing craft. The Campbells were a grand family, very warm and hospitable . They lived in the house on the island and looked after the cattle that were shipped over to graze in the summer, while in the winter they repaired the dykes and gates and looked after shooting parties which came over for the weekend. Young Bill Jacobs, the head-keeper's son, and I stayed with the Campbells in their house while Sir Joseph and his guests lived in a wooden cabin built on the end. Bill and I shared a double brass bed in the Campbell's sitting room. I am afraid that we did not get much sleep because the mattress on the bed was flock, full of large lumps. It was probably more uncomfortable for Bill than for me for I am one of Pharaoh's lean kine, able to curl between the lumps but Bill, being of more ample proportions, could only lie on top of them.

If the bed was not bad enough, in the corner of the room stood an ancient grandfather clock, one of Jock's family heir-looms, so he said; it chimed every quarter of an hour and struck a gong on the half hour and the hour. No sooner did it recover from one part before it started wheezing and groaning, building itself up for its next onslaught. I think the clock and the mattress vied with each other to make sure we had little sleep.

On the south side of the island, between the sea wall and the edge of the river, was a stretch of Greenshore, full of small

freshwater pools and little creeks, around which grew sweet grass and lots of Michaelmas daisy. There were always lots of ducks feeding on the grass, wash-ing and brushing up in the pools along with hundreds of snipes which fed there, probing among the daisies. In the after-

noon, just before evening flight, Jock would take a couple of the guns down to the far end of the Greenshore on the tractor-drawn sledge. The guns would wait in a hide and Bill and I would drive the snipe towards them. When the birds were disturbed, they would fly down the Greenshore, which was about one hundred and fifty to two hundred yards wide, and they made some lovely sporting shots. We seldom shot many but fired a good number of cartridges and it filled in an empty hour before the duck flight.

I remember one afternoon when Sir Joseph told me to take an extra bag of cartridges and have a few shots as I was walking down. There were many more snipe that day than usual and I started banging away with gay abandon and, although I fired numerous cartridges, I did not bag many snipe. At the time, I thought they were either very difficult to hit or I was shooting very badly. The next morning I found out that I had picked up the wrong bag of cartridges by mistake and had been using 3-inch No.1 shot intended for geese. No wonder I did not hit the snipe.

The dog that Sir Joseph owned was getting on in years and was pensioned off, so he bought a new one, named Don, the best dog in water I have ever seen in my life. Don started his career in the game-shooting field but, at eighteen months of age, far too early in his first season, he was sent out to retrieve and fell foul of a very bad-tempered older dog who gave him a good hiding. As is so often the case when this happens to a young dog, Don became a fighter; he never waited to be attacked again, he made sure he got in first. He was so bad that he could not be taken anywhere where he was likely to meet other dogs. Don was banned from the game-shooting field and only allowed to go with us to Read's Island. He really excelled himself at wildfowling for he loved the water.

I once saw him go out into the River Humber at flood tide after a goose that was able to flap along on the top of the water; as the goose struggled further out, Don followed; he would not be called off. The tide was running at a tremendous rate and, after a while, they both disappeared into the dusk. I thought we would never see either of them again and we walked the shore line calling and calling and, after what seemed an eternity, we heard Don snorting and puffing ashore, well down toward the other end of the island. A little later, he proudly brought back the goose. This was the bravest and best retrieve I have ever witnessed in my life and it just goes to show to what lengths a good dog will go to please his master. Sir Joseph thought it a shame to keep him just for a few days' wildfowling so he gave him to my brother whom he accompanied to sea, whelking. Don reigned supreme over the saltings wildfowling for there were no other dogs in the harbour for him to fight, so it was a perfect life for him. When I went home for a holiday in the summer months, Don loved to come with me butt-pricking. He would swim alongside as I was working up the main channel where the water flows swiftly about three feet deep and, every so often, he would dive to the bottom and retrieve an oyster shell.

Unfortunately Don met an untimely end. He had been with my brother for about three years and had learned that it was just as nice to please some of the lady dogs in the village as it was his master. He took to sneaking off at every opportunity. Don was returning home from an evening's courting, crossed the road in front of a car and was killed instantly; it was such a pity and such a waste.

Jock Campbell awoke one morning to find Read's Island

crawling with water voles, thousands upon thousands of which had swum over from the mainland during the night. There were so many that, in the evening when they were active, it looked as though the whole marsh was moving: if you sent a dog to retrieve a duck he would usually come back with a live water vole. This plague was quickly followed by a large number of kestrels which preyed on the rats; you could often count up to thirty of them hovering at one time, a lovely sight. It is amazing how a kestrel can kill, lift and fly off with a water vole, which probably weighs twice as much as the bird. If we sat quietly on the sea wall, a kestrel would hover within a few yards of us: watching them at close quarters through binoculars, it is remarkable to see how they maintain their position by gathering the wind and spilling it out again by the use of their tail and flight feathers: I would recommend anyone to watch these lovely little falcons when they are hovering, for they would receive an unforgettable lesson in aerodynamics.

The water voles did very serious damage by burrowing holes into the dykes and ditches and then they started on the sea wall. This was a great worry because the wall was only a bank of soil grassed over and, if the voles riddled it with holes, the sea could easily breach the wall and flood the whole island. Bill Jacobs (the head keeper), Jimmy Needs and myself spent many days over on the island with our terriers trying to get rid of some of the voles. The terriers killed hundreds and hundreds, and we used every method we could think of, but to no avail; we just did not make any impression on them. Finally, after about three years, they disappeared as quickly as they came and the kestrels went with them. Nature is sometimes very strange in her ways. What should cause those voles to swim across a wide expanse of tidal water and then, after a few years, disappear so suddenly? I would love to know the answer.

Over the years, I have seen correspondence in various sporting magazines about hares swimming across rivers and

lakes. It was in my first season at Rothwell that we netted alive a large number of hares and set them free on Read's Island, hoping they would breed and establish themselves, but in two years they had all swum back across the water and not a hare was left on the island. I have also seen hares swim across the harbour at Brancaster Staithe when the tide was in, so hares are far stronger swimmers than we realise. We normally see them in the environment of ploughed fields and woodland or loping across a large stubble, so it is difficult to imagine the same animals swimming across a large expanse of salt water.

However, I think at the end of the day, my first love will always be the grey partridge, such wonderful little birds which respond well to a little care and attention. There is an old saying among partridge keepers that, if you keep the predators down to a reasonable level, the partridge will look after itself. When you visit a nest and see the hen sitting tight and motionless, or the cock bird, faithfully standing on guard with his head stretched as high as possible and his tail flicking up and down while his mate has just come off the nest to feed, or to see them both brooding and fussing over their chicks, these sights are reward enough for all the tramping up and down the hedgerows visiting the tunnel traps, nests and all the hundred and one duties that are part of a partridge-keeper's life.

It is surprising what can be done with a partridge nest if one is very careful and patient. I found a partridge scrape one day and when I looked a couple of days later she had started to lay. All went well until she had laid six eggs at which time a French partridge started to lay in the same nest. The normal procedure when this happens is to keep taking the French bird's eggs out of the nest, to visit the nest as often as possible and vary the times as much as possible, trying to catch the intruder on the nest and give her a good fright to make her desert. Hopefully, she will then go off and make a nest of her own. This particular nest was on a lovely sunny bank facing south, such a nice place that I decided to try a little experiment. I made up a dummy nest about two feet away and put the French bird's three eggs in it. Next day when I visited, the French bird had laid again in the English bird's nest so I moved that egg also. The same thing happened again the following day, but when the French hen came to lay her sixth egg, to my delight she laid them in the dummy nest. I waited until she had laid two more eggs in the same nest and then I moved the nest and eggs away from the English hen's nest, very carefully choosing a new site as similar to the old one as possible. She continued to lay, so I moved the nest again and again until eventually I had moved her about five or six yards. I thought I should leave well alone because she would soon be coming to the incubation period.

Both the English and French partridge went down on their eggs on the same day and sat quite happily a short distance from one another right up to the twentieth day of incubation. On the twenty-first day I again visited the nests when I saw to my horror that the French bird's nest was covered by an old sack. She had deserted, of course, and she never returned. I found out later that, shortly after my visit to the nests on the twentieth day, the shepherd had gone up the grass track in his pony and cart past the sitting birds when a sack must have fallen off the back of the cart. On his return, the pony had shied at the sack so the shepherd picked it up and threw it on to the bank, right on top of the nest. He had no way of knowing there was a nest there and went on his way. If only I had been a couple of hours later on my visit I could have saved the clutch, especially at that late stage of incubation. The English bird hatched successfully a few days later. I have moved nests in this way quite a few times since then and the operation has proved successful.

The reason we remove the pheasants' and French partridge eggs from an English partridge's nest is that, although they  have the same twenty-four day incubation period, the larger pheasant eggs will be kept at the correct temperature but will lift the brooding bird slightly higher off the partridge eggs, which are thus kept at a slightly lower temperature and patch a day or so later. Pheasant and partridge will brood on the nest only until the chicks have dried off after hatching, about twelve hours, before they move off with their broods into the surrounding fields. Thus the partridge eggs, which might have hatched a day later, are left in the nest. It was said by those keepers and guns who loved their partridge shooting that you needed good weather during Royal Ascot week. This is absolutely correct but I like to see nice weather a week before and the week after, because that is when the bulk of the birds hatch and, if they can get off to a good start, half of your troubles are over.

There are two critical stages in a partridge chick's life. If the weather turns wet and cold just as they hatch, it will wipe out the young birds for that season. The other time is when they are a fortnight to three weeks old, as the parent birds cannot cover and protect all the poults, particularly if there are many of them. Some of them have to sit on the outside and can become thoroughly wet and chilled. In their efforts to find some warmth and shelter, the outside ones push their way under the old bird and force some of the drier ones out so they also catch a chill.

As I go round the estate, I take note of where there is a covey and also make a mental record of the numbers of young. When conditions are wet and cold for twenty-four hours or longer, I see the covey gradually dwindling, the young poults dying a week after getting thoroughly chilled. In modern agriculture, most of the acreage is down to cereal and there is not much shelter for young game birds, such as they can find under the broad leaves of root crops such as mangolds. Also there are now few meadows and hayfields that used to give the game birds an opportunity to get away from the wet, cold soil, which is picked up and clogs their feet. Old turf also holds a great variety of insect life which, due to spraying, is not found in corn fields.

After I had spent five years at Rothwell, I felt it was time I moved on and gained some experience on a pheasant estate. I heard of an under keeper's job at Clarendon Park in Wilt-shire, went for interview and was offered the situation. I had saved a little money and bought, for £15, our first car. We felt like the owners of a Rolls Royce in our 1932 Austin 10 with an engine which ran like a stag, brakes which worked sometimes and a roof  which leaked. She took us safely from Lincolnshire to Wilt-shire, my wife holding an umbrella to keep us dry, and we stopped every forty miles or so to top up the radiator from roadside puddles. We arrived safely amid a cloud of steam to begin a new chapter in our lives.

# 4 · Clarendon Park

Clarendon Park lies on the south side of Salisbury in Wiltshire and the partridge beat that I looked after commanded some lovely views of Salisbury Cathedral. It is a wonderful sporting estate, for not only was there a good quantity of game, but the quality of the sport was very high indeed. At that time, Clarendon was owned by Major Christie Miller, a first-class gentleman: I believe that his son Andrew has now taken the reins. The Major's father laid out much of the estate, planting main belts of trees on the high ground and narrow belts running away from them, separating the fields, better than hedges.

On pheasant-shooting days, about four beaters, with a keeper or one of the forestry men in charge, carefully drove the narrow belts, pushing the birds into the main woods then waiting for the rest of the beaters to work their way down to them. We had five drives in any one day and the birds were very high indeed; we shot with six guns. The Major never stood with his guests, preferring to walk with the beaters to catch those cunning old cock birds that developed the habit of breaking back. The belts were also designed for showing excellent partridges.

Jack Dorling was head keeper, a first-class man and also a very good naturalist. You could show him any variety of wild flower or grass or any kind of bird and he would tell you its name. There were six keepers there at that time: I was partridge keeper and all the others were pheasant men, although Bill Dawes, my neighbouring beat keeper, had a few hundred acres of partridge ground. Bill was a grand character, one of nature's gentlemen. He had a stiff leg, a legacy of the 1914–1918 war but this did not hinder him in any way. He could walk over plough or through the brambles with the best of us. The Major thought the world of Clarendon, especially the forestry and game departments and he seemed happiest when he was mixing and yarning with the keepers. He met me one day as I was walking round my beat and said, 'Those film people are not having any luck with that magpie's nest they are trying to film. They have been sitting in their hide off and on for a fortnight, but the old birds have not yet returned to the nest'. I asked him if he meant the magpie's nest on the other side of Gilbert's Wood, where it looked as if some children had built a hut out of sacks. 'Yes', he said, 'but that hut is the hide the film people have made'. I told him they would not have much luck because I had shot those mag-pies nearly three weeks ago. I thought the Major was going to burst himself he laughed so much.

The partridge beat I took over had not been shot for many years and was sadly neglected, being infested with rats and other predators. There was a poultry farm on my beat and this harboured the rats. Another young keeper, my son Rodney and I went out night after night with our two terriers. I had a fantastic little bitch terrier named Sally and we used to kill up to eighty rats a night around the poultry houses. I used a great quantity of poison and also trapped a great many: it took me about three months to get rid of them.

One of the woods on the edge of my beat was named The Graves. In this wood was a plot of consecrated ground where the Major's father was buried and also a memorial for his brother who had been killed in action during the Normandy landings. The grass was always beautifully cut during the summer and the hedges neatly trimmed. There was a grand view across the valley with the city of Salisbury and its lovely Cathedral on the far side of the valley. I walked through The Graves Wood most days and seldom did I miss the opportunity to walk to the hedge at the end and take advantage of such a lovely scene. This wood was never shot, but was treated as a sanctuary. The Major said his late father would be delighted if he could have seen all those pheasants running over his grave. I often fed up two hundred birds in The Graves Wood, most of them hens. It is funny how hen pheasants seem to prefer some woods to others and do so year after year. It is not because these particular 'hen woods', as we call them, are warmer than others because, on my current estate, I have one that lies on a slope with the prevailing wind blowing right into it, so it is quite cold in the winter.

An amusing thing happened in the first year at Clarendon. Thousands of starlings decided to roost in Savage's Belt, a lovely young wood, and it was imperative that we got them to move before they killed the wood as I had seen them do at Rothwell. We spent three nights shooting at them, but it made not the slightest difference. Then we went to the fireworks factory on Salisbury Plain for a demonstration and came home with a hundred big Roman candles. These we stuck in the soft earth down the centre ride. It was our intention to let them off just as the starlings were about to settle for the night and try to frighten them away. We also placed several fifty-gallon drums of diesel-soaked sacks along the windward side of the wood. If the fireworks did not frighten the birds, we thought we might smoke them out. We waited patiently, our guns, smoke, fireworks and matches at the ready, but the starlings did not come to roost that night or ever again. A week or so later we had our own private firework display. I had Bisto, my black labrador dog, with me when we let the fireworks off and he did not seem to understand that there was all this banging and no retrieving for him to do.

Dogs play a very important part in a keeper's life for there are so many things a good one can do more quickly and more efficiently than the keeper. I have been very lucky in my life to have owned some really good ones. You only have one really outstanding dog in your life and mine was a little long-haired mongrel terrier named Sally. I seldom went out without her and one of my regrets  is that I did not keep a record of the rats and rabbits we caught together. Jimmy Needs bred her from his two terriers, Tinker and Patch, at Rothwell and I bought Sally for a packet of Woodbines. She killed her first rat when she was three months old and bolted her first fox when she was only seven months. I had just over one hundred tunnel traps on my beat and she knew where each one was and saved me many miles of walking. If I did not want to go down a particular hedge because it was out of my way, Sally would trot off, look at the tunnel trap at the other end and if there was anything in the trap she would kill it if it was not already dead and stay and bark for me to come to reset the trap. If there was nothing in it, she would just come back to me and we would go on our way.

During my early days at Clarendon, there were many rats around the poultry fields. As I was on my way home for lunch one day, I found a place where the hedge had been pulled out and the chickens had scratched the loose soil level, like a giant furrow running down the hill across the field. In this depression, there were hundreds of rat holes. Nearby was a hose pipe connected to a water tap. I put the end of the hose pipe in the top hole, turned on the tap and went home for my lunch. Sally and I came back about an hour later to find all the holes at the top of the slope flooded and the rats concentrated in the lower holes. We stayed there most of the afternoon, Sally killing the rats as quickly as they were flooded out. When it was obvious that none were left I counted the bag, eighty-six, and Sally had killed the lot by herself.

On shooting days, she would hunt and retrieve like the best pedigree gun dog and a good deal better than many I had seen. Not only was she the perfect working dog but when we came home she was the perfect pet, quite happy to be dressed up in doll's clothes and be pushed about in a pram by my daughter. She went with us to Clarendon and to my present place at Tetworth, where she died, aged twelve, having actually worked on the day she died. I buried her on my rearing field; I often talk about her; I am afraid most of my dogs are measured against her and you just can't beat perfection.

After 1st May, when the partridges started to lay, I spent most of my daylight hours searching for nests and as I was concerned that there might be a few rats I had missed, I decided to Euston System all the nests. I persuaded Jack Dorling to exchange five hundred eggs with a head-keeper friend from an estate fifty miles away; the idea was to change and to improve the blood line of our partridge stock. That year we had a marvellous season and, although I lost a few pheasant nests, I hardly lost a partridge that was sitting on dummy eggs. After they had been incubating for fourteen to eighteen days, I gave each hen seventeen chipped eggs (I always believe in an odd number) and every hen accepted them. This dodge, coupled with a very kind summer, paid dividends. The birds hatched and reared very well indeed and, on my first day's shooting, we killed one hundred and thirty-five and a half brace to seven guns.

There were many cattle on the other side of the estate and silage and hay was made. The keepers on this beat searched the fields for nests and any partridge eggs that they found they brought to me. Some of these I used in my Euston programme and the surplus I hatched and took to a rearing field behind Bill Dawes' house; Bill and I helped each other to rear them. Hand-rearing English partridges is much more rewarding than pheasant-rearing. The rearing field was at the foot of a Wiltshire 'hanging', as it was called, and was a mass of ant hills, a perfect place for young partridges. Bill lived in an ex-army Nissen hut converted to a lovely home by a high-ranking German officer prisoner of war who was billeted there. It had oak beams, a lovely stone fireplace and French windows. It had been built into the side of a steep bank and it was along the top of this bank, which was level with the roof of the hut, that we walked to and from the rearing field. We were on our way back from the field for our lunch, Bill carrying a large bantam which had just killed her eighteen partridge chicks and because of this he was in a very bad mood.

When we reached his house, his wife Frances came out and said, 'Bill, when are you going to sweep that so and so chimney? You have been promising for weeks now and still have not done it'. Bill never said a word and Frances continued grumbling. Able to stand it no more, Bill stepped from the bank onto the roof of the Nissen hut and dropped the bantam down the chimney. When we went round through the French windows, there sat the bantam clucking away in the fireplace and the whole of the room was covered in soot. Bill picked up the bird, tucked her under his arm and, as he stomped out  through the French windows, said to a now speechless Frances, 'There you are, woman; that's swept your bloody chimney'. Needless to say, we did not get any coffee and biscuits for a few mornings after that.

The ant hills on our rearing field had been there for many years and were quite large, some of them were more than eighteen inches high. We developed the knack of gently moving the pen, with the bantam and her brood of partridge chicks, close to an ant hill and then quickly lifting the pen over it. As soon as the bantam saw the ants she would rush onto the hill and start scratching and calling to her chicks, who were never slow to join in; they really loved ant eggs and I am sure this is one of the reasons we were able to get such good rearing results. When the chicks were old enough, we took each bantam and her brood and put them on various parts of the estate as far apart as possible.

Over the years, we tried every means that we could devise of releasing the young partridges but, each year, after a few weeks apart, they assembled in large packs which, unlike a wild covey, seemed to have no sense of home but would range far and wide over the estate. It was quite common to see one of the packs somewhere in the morning and see them again in the afternoon one and a half miles away; often they left the estate, never to return. The strange thing was that, although we had large shooting estates all around us, we never received word that someone had a new pack of English partridges on his ground; I often wonder where they went; someone benefited from them even if we did not.

In my last year rearing at Clarendon, I tried a new experiment. I picked out twenty-five young hen partridges and kept them all winter; at the end of March, I put out twenty-five pens in different places, a hen in each, the pens spread out over Bill Dawes' beat and mine. I visited the pens each day and, after they had been out a week, I noticed a wild cock bird running away from each pen as I approached. I left my birds in the pens until I was sure that they each had attracted a mate and then, one night after dark, I walked round and quietly opened each little trap door and, at first light next morning, the hens were able to go out and join their husbands. I had painted a small patch of red dye on the backs of each hen so that I could recognise them through my binoculars. My theory was that, if I released the hens late in the spring, they would be desperate to mate and nest and the wild cocks would act as anchors. This worked very well and I saw most of the hens for several weeks after their release and knew that most of them nested on the estate. It was a very worthwhile experiment but I did not have the opportunity to try it again.

The woodcock arrive in great numbers during October and

November. They fly across the North Sea and fall exhausted into the sand dunes and can be easily picked up they are so tired. The older men used to tell us boys that the woodcock always carried a piece of stick in his beak when he flew across the sea and, if we were fool enough to ask why, we were told it was so that he could stand on it in the water and have a rest. The woodcock remain in the sand dunes for a few days, gathering their strength after their long flight, then they move on to other parts of the country for the winter.

I was walking through The Graves Wood when I spotted a slight movement on the ground; after staring at that spot for a short time, I gradually picked out the outline of a hen wood-cock sitting on a nest, quite in the open, surrounded by leaves. The sitting woodcock is the prettiest and best-camouflaged bird I know. I have been lucky in my life to have found two sitting woodcock. I showed this nest to Jack Dorling who told me that, although he started with his father, who was a head keeper for as long as he could remember, he had never had the pleasure of finding a woodcock's nest and he was then sixty-four years of age. I used this path nearly every day, and sometimes twice a day, yet I had not seen her before due to her amazing

camouflage. The incubation period of a woodcock is twenty-two to twenty-four days so I must have passed her at least twenty times because the eggs hatched two days after I had found her.

There has been regular correspondence in various shooting magazines about whether or not woodcock carry their young. I suspected that they did so because, when I had seen the young ones run to their mother, she flew away, as I thought, carrying them between her thighs. There was always room for doubt; it was possible that the young could have hidden in the grass or sneaked away through the leaves. However, on three separate occasions over the last few years, in the presence of my son, I have seen a woodcock on absolutely bare ground with her two young, twice on the site of an old bonfire and once on bare ground in the woods. From about twenty-five yards range, we saw the two young run to their mother; after a few seconds she flew heavily away, with her legs half dangling and what appeared to be one lump on each thigh. There was no possible way those chicks could have been moved off that bare ground without them being carried. There is no doubt in my mind that woodcock do carry their young when danger threatens.

There were many birds at Clarendon that I have not seen since I left, among them the corncrake, crossbill, stone curlew and red-backed shrike. On a nice sunny day, we could see up to a dozen buzzards riding a thermal, wheeling higher and higher until they were specks in the sky. It is a well-known fact that there is a greater wealth of bird life on a well-keepered estate than on one where there is no keeper because we control the predators to help the game birds and the other birds benefit also.

Some birds, like the lapwing, skylark and stone curlew that nest on the ground in open fields, have been very hard hit by changes in farming. Years ago, when the corn was a few inches high, the field gate was shut and not re-opened until harvest but, nowadays, the farmer seems to be forever treating the corn with something or other right through nesting time. In those

days, there were large acreages on most
estates that the farmer was unable to cultivate
but nowadays, with his larger machinery and
powerful fertilisers, there are not many of
these places left. When I go home to Norfolk,
I see men cultivating large fields which, when
I was a boy, were one mass of whins and
bracken. I have seen vast changes in agriculture during my lifetime, from the horse to the
high-powered tractor, but farming is forever

changing and, who knows, I might yet see the grey partridge
make a comeback to its numbers of forty years ago.

The wood next to The Graves Wood was called The Ruins,
which took its name from the ruins of the old Clarendon Castle
around which, over the years, the wood had been allowed to
grow. The castle must have been an enormous place in its
heyday, covering at least eight acres and parts of it have been
preserved. The walls were about five feet high when I last saw
them, so I was able to gain an idea of what it used to be like. In
my first year, some archaeological excavating was done and I
spent much more time with the team of excavators than I
should have done. When the professor in charge found that I
was interested in his work, he explained to me how the castle
had been when it was last occupied, showing me the sites of the
great hall, the bedrooms, servants' quarters and kitchens. As he
was explaining all this, I could almost see the colourful people
who lived there going about their everyday lives. I was very
fortunate to have had this glimpse into the past. They unco-
vered an inlaid tiled floor, a very important find, and also the
kiln which fired the tiles. This floor went to the British
Museum but I had one of the tiles for many years and used it as
a teapot stand; sadly it was eventually broken and thrown away.

One day, as I was walking towards an old chalk pit on the
edge of my beat, I smelt wood smoke. I peeped over the edge
and saw that a family of gypsies had moved in; I guessed they
must have been the same family I had been warned to watch out

for, well-known poachers who had been a thorn in the side of previous keepers sides for many years. I had already made up my mind that, when they came to camp again, as they did two or three times a year, I would try a new approach. I went off and shot a brace of hares and a couple of rabbits, came back from a different direction, walked up to their camp fire and introduced myself as the new keeper. I chatted to them for ten or fifteen minutes and, as I was about to leave, I asked them if they would like the rabbits and hares I had in my bag. They readily accepted and seemed very grateful. Over the next few years I did the same kind of thing every time I saw them and I also had some very interesting conversations with them. I checked carefully around my beat after they had visited but never saw any signs of poaching. A fortnight before I left Clarendon to come to Tetworth, the gypsies were in the chalkpit again so I went and said goodbye to them and told them I was leaving for another job. The old man said, 'Thank you for being so kind and friendly towards us; we used to poach the estate before you came but we have never touched a thing while you have been here'. My idea paid off, so it sometimes pays to take a fresh approach to a problem. That family were the genuine Romany gypsies, not many of whom are about today. I enjoyed the conversations I had with them for they seemed to have a wonderful way with birds and animals and their customs and outlook on life were so different from what I was used to. I am sure I learned much from them and came away the richer for having known them. I often wonder what happened to the keeper who took over my beat when I left and if he had any trouble from them.

On pheasant-shooting days at Clarendon, my job was picking up behind the guns. I had a very good brace of black labradors, Gaye and Bisto, and it gave me a chance to work with dogs, which I loved. Gaye was a very useful bitch who liked to work close, but the strength of the team was Bisto. He would never have won a prize for his looks at a dog show, but he could certainly find game. He was the best picking-up dog I have ever owned, so clever that he seemed to know where wounded birds would make for and head straight for the spot. Several times during a day's shooting I was asked to look for a bird that the other dogs could not find and Bisto nearly always retrieved it. Some of the guns joked that I told Bisto whether it was a cock or a hen I wanted and he went off and caught an un-shot bird of the correct sex. The Major used to say that if Nudds and Bisto could not find the bird, it was a waste of time any other dog trying. Bisto's only weakness, for which I always forgave him, was hares. When we walked across a field and hares jumped up around our feet he would look at me as if to say, 'I would never dream of chasing a hare', but many was the time I stood on the top of a ride in a wood when Bisto was working and he thought I could not see him and I would see a hare cross the bottom of the ride as fast as he could go with Bisto hard on his heels. I suppose the best of us has his faults.

The Major told me a lovely story concerning the old head keeper, Mr Lamdon, who had retired just as I went to Clarendon. The Major had finished college and had seen nearly two seasons shooting and thought he knew all there was to know about driving out woods. He thought they should drive Gilbert's Wood in a different and more productive way. He spoke about this to Mr Lamdon but he would not even listen so he went to his father, was firmly put in his place and told that Mr Lamdon was the head keeper and he would always do his utmost to ensure that birds would be presented to the best of his ability. The guns had the best sport available and he was forbidden to interfere again. Many years later, when his father died and the Major took over, he thought he would have his own way at last, so, when Gilbert's Wood was due to be shot, he went to Mr Lamdon and this time he listened attentively and enquired where the Major thought the drive should start and where he would place the guns. He thought carefully for a few minutes before saying, 'A jolly good idea, Mr Sam; you place your guns where you said but I am still going to drive the wood the same way as I always do because that is the way the birds fly the highest'. The Major never argued with him again after that. You have a job to beat a good professional for, in my first year, we drove Gilbert's Wood the way the Major had wanted all those years before. It was a complete fiasco but the Major seemed pleased that he had been proved wrong.

Clarendon House had a wonderful wild garden which had been laid out by the Major's mother. It was one of the finest of its kind I have ever seen. Walking across the park was more like walking into a wood but, directly you were in and following one of the many paths that wound their way among the bushes, trees and shrubs, you encountered breath-taking panoramic views and every time you rounded a bend you encountered a different scene. It is a wonderful gift to have the foresight to create something like that from open parkland. I took every opportunity of walking through the wild garden and, every time I did so, I enjoyed it as much as the first time I ever saw it. There was something in flower every day of the year.

About twice a year, we had to drive the gardens to try to thin out the rabbits which lived among the rhododendrons. We were not allowed to use sticks or guns and had to be especially careful where we trod in case we damaged any plants. We ran some long nets around the paths, mustered every dog we could to chase the rabbits into nets and, as could be expected, we often had one rabbit, two or three dogs plus a couple of keepers all in the nets at the same time. We enjoyed ourselves, the dogs had a whale of a time, but the rabbit population did not suffer very much at all.

During the spring and summer months, a keeper does most good before seven in the morning and after seven at night. It is grand to be about in those few hours just after daybreak when nature has everything to herself before man starts to disturb the quietness of the countryside with his noisy machines. At that time in the morning, the birds and animals do not expect to be disturbed by man and seem quite tame. I have walked up unnoticed to an old boar badger who was rooting up the earth, searching for tasty morsels in a patch of bluebells. I stood and watched him for a short time until some sense told him that there was something wrong and he trundled off into the undergrowth. I have often seen a fox cutting across a grass field on his way home from his night's excursion. He will suddenly stop, freeze, lift his head as high as possible, take two or three stiff-legged springing jumps and pounce on a mouse. Sometimes he will stand absolutely motionless, like a pointer dog, with one foot raised and his head cocked on one side then, all of a sudden, he will pounce and dig furiously. After a few seconds, he will kill the mole he had heard working underground.

Walking down a hedgerow, you may see a bitch stoat coming towards you in the process of moving her young from one place to another. Put your hand on a table with your thumb and fingers touching each other and that's how close the bitch and the young ones are, for all the world as though they were glued together: as mum turns, they all turn.

One lovely summer's night, I was walking by the side of a field of barley that had been cut and the straw baled when

I noticed that some of the bales had been gathered up and made into a house. I expected it was some of the children from the village and thought I would have a game with them. I crept quietly up to the straw house and could hear whispering voices from inside so I gave the bales a mighty push. To my surprise, a partially-dressed man and girl jumped up, they young lady wearing only a small vest; she recognised me immediately, grabbed the hem of her vest and pulled it up to hide her face. This amusing incident happened nearly thirty years ago but I still can't remember much about that girl's face!

Jack Dorling came to see me one day and asked me if I would take Bisto and go and help one of his head-keeper pals, who had a day's shooting arranged and was short of beaters. The estate was Lady Janet Baily's at Durnfors, where Harry Grass was the head keeper. I learned a lot that day, watching how Harry drove his birds, maneouvring his beaters and using the wind to get the birds to fly a bit higher and faster. It was a useful experience for me because, until that time, I had only seen pheasants driven straight out of the end of the wood and not shown to their best advantage. Harry Grass came from a very well-known family of keepers, a very large man, but like most big men a very kind and gentle person, unless someone was foolish enough to arouse him. Shortly after I met him, he moved to Broadlands as head keeper to the late Earl Mountbatten. Harry had a lot of bother from poachers in his first season at Broadlands. One day he caught two men in the act and, when he asked them to accompany him to the police station, they put up a fight. Harry grabbed them both by the scruff of their necks, banged their heads together and laid them both out.

One of the things that impressed me much about Harry Grass was that he had learned his trade by starting at the bottom and, during his life, had gained a vast knowledge of nature and the gamekeeper's duties, yet he was always ready to give the benefit of his experience to anyone who went to him for advice. Our profession is the poorer when men like him retire.

We were shooting Cecil Lane's beat one day at Clarendon when everyone had a good laugh at the expense of one of the Major's guests. Accompanied by a new dog, he arrived at Clarendon Hall and was introduced to the other guns, when the Major remarked that he hoped this dog was more steady than the previous dogs he had brought. The guest extolled the virtues of his new one, how it came from a long line of field-trial champions, could swim like an otter, find a pheasant anywhere, was absolutely rock steady to rabbits and hares and would not run in. Just before lunch, we were shooting a long wood that ran along on the side of a steep bank with a meadow down in the valley in the bottom, in which was a herd of large white breeding sows. The wood was half moon-shaped so, as you walked, you could not see more than thirty yards behind. The Major sent the guest and his new dog to act as walking gun on the side of the wood, with strict instructions to keep up with the beaters and to leave any pheasants he shot until the end of the drive and then go back and pick them up.

As the birds left the wood, they came very high and fast, heading straight out over the valley. The guest was an excellent shot and he managed to account for eight, which fell way down in the valley bottom, and, as he disappeared round the curve of the wood, the sows rushed up and gobbled the lot. Everyone in the shooting field except that one man knew exactly what

would happen to a dead pheasant that fell in the sows' meadow. After the drive, he went back as instructed but returned empty-handed and has his leg pulled mercilessly. He was told his new dog was no good but must be blind and have no sense of smell. The Major gave me a wink, told his friend to never mind but Nudds would take Bisto back to find them. Off we went and, when we were out of sight round the corner, there was one of the beaters ready for me with eight pheasants; the Major had sent him back round the other side of the wood. I waited for ten minutes before returning with the birds and, as I arrived, the Major remarked casually, 'It's seldom old Bisto lets us down'. I often wonder if that gentleman ever learned what really happened.

I once saw a spectacular sight when we were shooting Roundabout Wood. The beaters had blanked in nearly a mile of Wiltshire 'hanging' into the wood which was not a very big one. I was standing back behind the guns, picking up as the beaters were blanking in and saw a great many birds running forward into the wood. Jack Dorling was experimenting with wire netting to make the pheasants take off at the top of the hill as, when they flew over the guns from the top, they came so high they were very testing. Beaters had barely entered the wood to start the drive when a fox came forward, ran down the length of the wire netting and sent out all the pheasants in one gigantic flush: there must have been at least five hundred birds in the air at the same time, a wondrous sight, but the drive was completely ruined. As 'Charles' emerged from the wood and trotted off across the field, he was given a rousing cheer by all the guns and beaters and followed by a few choice words from the other keepers.

When Bill Dawes left Clarendon to take up a head-keeper position on the Isle of Wight, a young man was engaged and placed under my supervision to train as a partridge keeper. I soon found out he was a lazy, useless person who, like so many more youngsters, thought the keeper's job was walking about dressed in a tweed suit, a pedigree dog at heel and a gun under his arm. I had him with me on the partridge-rearing field but he was so unreliable I found out the surest way to get things done was to do them myself. Towards the end of the partridge season, Jack Dorling asked me if I could spare Bob, as he intended to put two hundred pheasant poults in Queen Eleanor Belt on his beat and he could look after them. I readily agreed as the lad was no help to me.

Bob had left me for about three weeks when Jack Dorling came to see me one day and asked my opinion of him. He believed that Bob was not feeding the young pheasants because there were not many of them left and he had not used much corn. He had visited the feed ride for several days running, at different times, but never actually seen Bob come and feed. When I told him that I had found the lad lazy and unreliable, Jack said that I should have spoken to him before. He was determined to find out if he was feeding the pheasants, and arranged to be at the end of the feed ride, from where he could see Bob's house, at six o'clock next morning; I would take over at one o'clock. I arrived on time and Jack said that Bob had not come to feed but, through his binoculars, had seen him come out of his house, cut a cabbage from the garden and go back indoors. I waited until four o'clock and was on the point of going home when I heard Bob's 500 Norton motorbike. There were only about a dozen pheasants left of the original two hundred released in the wood and, when they heard the motorbike, they went running down the ride to meet it. A short time later, Bob appeared at the end of the ride, his bag of corn on his petrol tank. He tore down the ride at about thirty miles an hour, scattering corn to the four winds, and three minutes later was back home, finished for the day. I stood open-mouthed in amazement. When Jack Dorling came to see me at home that evening and I told him what had happened, I thought he would have a fit, he was so cross. He went to Bob's house and gave him notice to finish immediately. It seems quite amusing now to think of those pheasants running after a motorbike for their food but we did not see the funny side of it at the time.

Clarendon Estate had about eight forestry workers in those days and they were a great help to us keepers, for they were all keen on wildlife and kept us informed of what they had seen whilst they were about their duties. When they worked in the young plantations at nesting time, they marked with a blazed stick any nest they had found and placed another stick in the ride pointing towards the nest so that, when we passed that way, we were able to find the place immediately. Sometimes there would be two or more hens laying in the nest, in which case we had to take the eggs and destroy the nest to make the hens build individual nests. On shooting days, the foresters were particularly useful: we were able to send any one of them off with a couple of beaters to blank in some hedgerows or a belt, knowing full well that the task would be done properly and that we would find them in the right place at the right time. Men like those are invaluable to a keeper who can only be in one place at a time and it is good to know that other people are helping as much as they can.

The beech trees at Clarendon are the most magnificent I have ever seen, really massive specimens. In the days of the cross-cut saw, it took two men four days to cut down and lop the branches off one of these giants, but the whole job was done in one day with a chain saw. Everyone was sorry when, due to age or some other factor, one of these great trees had to be felled. Old Fraser, the head forester, retired and a new man fresh from college took over: he told the Cross brothers, two of the old foresters, that their ideas were out-dated. They were planting a beech plantation at that time and he sent some of the foresters on ahead to make shallow holes with mattocks. The others followed behind, putting beech mast in the holes and filling them in. They finished the plantation in one day and the new head forester said, 'There you are; that's twice as quick'. Directly the men had gone home, the pheasants came out and, by the following evening they had eaten all the beech mast, so back the foresters had to come and plant young trees in the old-fashioned way.

There was a large acreage of woodland at Clarendon and we had many deer, mostly roe and fallow. These had to be thinned out every year because they did so much damage to the young trees, damage which had to be seen to be believed. Whole plantations were ruined in a few nights, resulting in not only the loss of a young wood but also the loss of several years growth; the trees may be replaced but the years cannot.

Culling deer is the only part of a gamekeeper's life that I do not like: I was always sorry when that time of the year came round, for deer are such lovely animals. It is wonderful to see them in the evening, peacefully feeding in the field by a wood, or to see a fallow stag with a fine head of antlers standing in a ride in the early morning with the mist up to his knees, the king of all he surveys. The keepers from nearby estates came and helped us to do this job and, in turn, we had to return their help, so the deer cull cost us several days a week during January and February.

When I had been at Clarendon for four years, I decided that it was about time I found myself a head-keeper's position. What I had in mind was to try and find either a shooting estate that had been run down in the game department or a new shoot just starting where I could put into practice the many things I had learned over the years. At the start of the 1959 shooting season, I told Jack Dorling and the Major what I wanted to do. They both thanked me very much indeed for what I had done over the past four years and promised to help me as much as they could in finding a new situation. In October, I heard that Sir Peter Crossman was looking for a gamekeeper for his Tetworth Hall Estate of three thousand acres. I applied for the job and, at my interview, I found that Tetworth was just what I had been looking for. The estate had been a good shoot years ago but had not been professionally keepered for some time so it would give me the ideal opportunity to put my many ideas into practice. The land was not ideal for game because of its heavy clay soil, which meant that, in a wet summer, wild pheasants and partridges would have a difficult time trying to rear their

young, but I liked the layout of the woods. Both my wife and I
fell in love with the old Victorian cottage that went with the job
and when I was offered the position I readily accepted.

# 5 · Tetworth Hall

We moved into the Keeper's Lodge at Tetworth Hall Estate on 1st January 1960. Our cottage had been the head keeper's house many years before when the estate had been a famous shoot; at one time there were sixteen keepers but of course, the estate was much larger in those days. Sir Peter and Lady Crossman are two wonderful people to work for and I have received every encouragement whenever I have gone to them with my suggestions or ideas to improve the sport on the estate. It is written in the Bible that no man can serve two masters; well I have done it for twenty-five very happy years and what is more, one of those masters is also a Master of Foxhounds.

While there was a good stock of partridges, mainly French, there were very few pheasants. People with dogs had been allowed to walk through the woods at will during the summer and the local poachers had taken their toll during the shooting season; the jay and grey squirrel population was very high. One of the first things I did was to get some straw and make some feed rides in the woods, because the weather was still cold and January is one of the worst times of the year for natural food and weed seeds. Any pheasants would be glad of a bit of extra food and I would be able to make an estimate of what stock I had left. When these rides had been fed regularly for a fortnight,

it was quite common to see as many as thirty grey squirrels but very few pheasants on my corn.

The guv'nor and I decided that the best thing to do in our first year was to buy in pheasant eggs and day-old chicks to rear and then shoot very lightly to make sure that we left a good stock. This would enable me, in the following years, to catch up the adult hens and produce our own eggs for a rearing programme. It also gave me a golden opportunity to stock the estate with the black-necked pheasant, which I think is the best of all the various breeds. A black-neck does not seem to stray like some of the others and, when it takes wing, it flies very strongly. Many shoots nowadays buy in day-old chicks or poults, but I prefer to produce and hatch our own eggs, believing that, if I select good specimen stock birds and look after them properly, they will lay good quality, fertile eggs which, in turn, will give strong healthy chicks which will grow into excellent, mature birds.

Our largest wood is Weavely Wood, just over a hundred acres in extent. Although it had some good rides, the wood was not liked by the wildlife and our first season shooting in Weavely was pretty disastrous. The wood is on very heavy, clay land and, due to its density, very little sunlight could get in, making it cold and dank. We decided that we could improve things by cutting a clearing through the middle and letting in the sunlight. A small patch was cut as an experiment in the first year, not only to see if the plan would work but also bearing in mind that the wood had been there for hundreds of years. If we rushed ahead and made a big clearing and things did not improve we could not put things back as they were. This factor must be uppermost in one's mind when undertaking a project of this kind.

The next year I was very pleased to see that the wildlife seemed to approve of what we had done and the following year the clearing was extended to six acres. Ever since it has been a lovely wood, a pleasure to walk through, for you never know what you will see next. What before had been bare earth and leaves under hazel and a few stunted oaks now flourished. A study group came and counted the plant life growing in the new

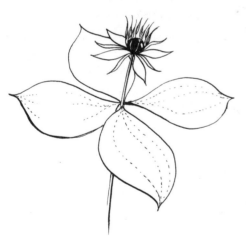

clearing and found that there were no less than eighty-seven different varieties, among which were some of the orchid family and the very rare herb Paris. The grasses and flowers attract thousands of butterflies. It goes to show that, when you try to help game by improving the habitat, other forms of wildlife benefit also.

Weavely Wood is open to the public at Easter weekend so they may come and see the masses of primroses and other flowers. I feel a great deal of satisfaction when I see the children with their baskets full of primroses and hear their happy voices, knowing that I have helped to create a small part of their enjoyment. Since the clearing was made and all those grasses and wild flowers have come up, some of them very rare, Weavely Wood has been declared a Site of Special Scientific

Interest. This would never have happened had it not been for the shooting and it just goes to prove that a properly-managed estate is vital for all forms of wildlife, as well as game. These days many people are conservation-minded, but estate-owners and gamekeepers have been conservationists for centuries, continually improving the game habitat by clearing an over-grown woodland, planting young trees, keeping rides clear and controlling predators. If this necessary work was not carried out, at considerable expense I might add, the woodlands would soon become overgrown and both game and song birds would suffer.

When I am planning to improve a particular pheasant drive, I give the subject a great deal of thought and look at all the possible different ways of doing it. If I reluctantly decide the only solution is to cut down a tree, I have the hardest task of all in persuading my governor to agree. When I first came to Tetworth, there was rather a wet meadow lying on the side of a steep hill behind the Hall. I stood on that spot one day and visualised pheasants flying from there back across the valley and I decided it would make a very good, sporting drive. I asked the governor if I could have a six-acre wood planted there and it took him all of five minutes to agree. It was planted that autumn and is now called The Larches and shows very sporting birds.

At about the same time, I asked for a tree to be cut down a very short distance from Red Grass Wood: it was making the birds divide when they left the wood, so that many of them turned back past the beaters and not over the guns because the tree was in the way. Fifteen years later I was still asking to have it removed and it was then cut down only because it was struck by lightning. I was accused by Lady Crossman of having placed a curse on the tree. It was a pollarded oak of lovely shape and from the outside appeared a perfect specimen but when it was cut down, only five inches around the outside was sound; the middle was rotten.

When I started rearing pheasants at Tetworth, I hatched half the eggs with broody hens and half with incubators. In those days, very few gamekeepers used incubators and my experience of them was very limited, but after a few years I learned more and had some very good results. We did away with the broodies and went for all incubators, which proved a wise decision, because it is now impossible to obtain broody hens in the quantity we need. My wife helped me with the job of taking the broody hens off their nests every morning so that they could feed and empty themselves; she enjoyed doing this and had names for most of them, although not very nice ones for those that killed her chicks as they hatched.

The keeper's wife has to be a very special kind of person. She has to help her husband, do lots of jobs and often has to clean up after muddy dogs and people who have tramped through her house. She acts as a nursemaid to sick dogs and other animals, puts up with hundreds of chicks round the Rayburn when heaters have failed on the rearing field, keeps meals hot when people call at inconvenient times and is frequently asked to do

'just a little feeding for me tomorrow'. She often acts as a 'stop' in the cold and rain of a shooting day, but when she has done these and many more things, she hears all the praise heaped on her husband's head and very little of it comes her way. She needs to be someone special to put up with all these things as well as her normal housewifely duties.

After I had been at Tetworth for five years, my son Rodney left school and joined me as under-gamekeeper. This extra help made a tremendous difference as we have been able to look after more release pens and spread our reared birds over the estate for, instead of releasing in three woods, we now release in six. This has also made our shooting days much better by giving us roughly the same size of bag each time we shoot; we can cater for three days without covering the same ground twice. Needless to say, the extra help is useful also on the rearing field. I have always believed in getting the  chicks onto grass at two days old and I have no time for brooder-house rearing.

If pheasants go straight onto grass, they build up a natural immunity to most diseases and they also grow accustomed to different temperatures at day and night so, when it is time for their move to the woods, they are hardened off properly. When birds are reared in sheds, they have drugs mixed in the food to prevent diseases and they never come into contact with ex-tremes of temperature or rain so that, when they are moved to the woods and suddenly are exposed to cold and wet, the losses can be great. Bill Jacobs at Rothwell was forever advising to keep as close to nature as possible.

After he has moved his pheasants to the wood, one of the keeper's biggest headaches is gapes. This is a parasitic worm that affects the poult's throat and, if it cannot cough it up, the bird slowly loses condition and dies. The poults catch it by eating earthworms and, on our wet clay soil at Tetworth, we get more than our share of gapes. I used to dread the weather turning to rain after we had moved the birds to wood, because I knew that would bring the earthworms up and, a week or so later, the poults would start 'snicking'. Years ago, keepers had their own ways of trying to cure the problem, but I think we must have killed more than we cured. We might put infected poults into a coop and then puff in lime so that they inhaled it, thus killing the worms. Another way was to push a feather soaked in turpentine or TCP down the bird's throat; such tricks seldom worked effectively, but it was pitiful to see your birds dying and not being able to help. About five years ago, a cure was found and now, when we hear that dreaded first 'snick', we are able to give the birds a dose of medicine and go to sleep at night without worrying how many we shall find dead in the morning.

We have quite a few badgers here at Tetworth. I have grown to love them more as I have grown older and at the moment we have five occupied setts. It is true that they take a few nests during the season, but in heavily wooded countryside like ours they do not great harm; I can always rear a few extra birds to offset losses to badgers. My son had a wonderful badger

experience a few years ago. One of the farmers was having trouble with pigeons eating his peas just as they were ripening in the pod. One afternoon, I sent Rodney to shoot some of them and he stood on the edge of an old sandpit close to where the badgers have a sett. He had been shooting for about and hour, when he heard a strange snuffling noise; he looked down and saw three badger cubs come out of a hole by his feet and start to play with each other. They romped around, came and sniffed at his shoes but otherwise totally ignored the fact he was there. He carried on shooting and killed over a hundred pigeons and all the time the cubs were playing about round his feet. I wish we had been able to photograph the event.

It makes me cross when I hear people refer to a badger that has killed some poultry or taken game-birds' nests as a 'rogue' badger. It is his natural instinct to eat flesh and, if one gets into a poultry house, he will take full advantage. In one year at Rothwell, I lost twelve nests in a single night to a badger. It had been raining during the night and I was able to track him from nest to nest and, as I came back onto the main road, two men in a car stopped and asked me if I was the gamekeeper. They introduced themselves as naturalists from Louth who were making a study of badgers and asked me to give my opinion of the animal. I'm afraid they got it, with a few extra words thrown in. After I had calmed down a bit, they told me I was wrong and that badgers do not take nests. I took them straight to the remains of a nest and pointed out the footmarks, they replied that in this case he must be a 'rogue' badger.

I have often thought about such incidents, for every year a badger came onto the estate and wandered up and down certain hedges, made for one of three favourite places where he would pull open an old rabbit hole and stay for just one or two days but seldom longer. He was always a young boar badger; had he, I wonder, been turned out of the sett by an older boar, and were the particular hedges he travelled old badger tracks of years ago, and were the rabbit holes they pulled open once old badger setts? Over the years, I have noticed, when a badger or a fox opens what appears to be a new earth, that if you take the trouble to enquire from some of the older men who have worked on the estate all their lives, they will be able to tell you they remember an earth or a sett being in the same place when they were children.

A man rang me to ask if he and some of his friends could come and study our badgers and record which setts were being used. When I politely refused but said I would be happy to give him any information he wanted regarding setts being used, he was not pleased and a week or so later wrote a letter on headed notepaper to my governor, almost demanding that he be allowed to come. I arranged to meet this person and asked him what he wanted to do. He wanted to sit and watch them, take dung samples to see what they were feeding on and fix up some lights in order to film them. I told him that I knew for certain that these badgers had been allowed to live their lives undisturbed for nearly twenty years and, until he could convince me that they might benefit from what he wanted to do, he would not be allowed to come and disturb them. Needless to say we have not heard from that group of people again. I think there is too much of this type of thing going on these days and I can't see how the birds and animals can benefit from such unwelcome disturbances. Are these people trying to help, or just satisfying their idle curiosity?

We always leave straw bales round the wood just after harvest to use later in the year for pheasants to scratch in when we begin feeding. When I was feeding a particular wood later in the year, I noticed that a badger had taken up residence in an old underground drain. I suspected he was an old boar turned out of a nearby breeding sett by his wife, who was probably about to have her young ones. I opened a fresh bale of straw for the pheasants to scratch in and, when I returned the next day, saw that the badger had turned out his old bed and taken in some of my clean straw. A few days later, I did the same thing and, sure enough, the badger once more changed his bedding at my expense. Having a warped sense of humour, I broke open fresh straw every day so that poor old brock was permanently engaged in changing his bed. He could not have had much time to feed, because he had to carry the straw about fifty yards.

Badgers will sometimes live quite happily in a sett for a great many years and then, for some reason best known to themselves, leave it and move to another which has been unoccupied perhaps for forty years. I think that they move because one of them may have died (possibly of disease) and their instinct tells them to move out for a time. I believe this because, when badgers open up an old sett or start digging in what appears to be a new part of an occupied one, they often dig out old bones and skulls of badgers that have died there years ago. I have looked at many of these skulls and I can tell by their teeth that they are sometimes the remains of young animals. What caused their death is a mystery. The skulls with well-worn molars most probably belong to badgers which died of old age. Often, when badgers open an old sett, there is no outward sign that there has been a hole there before. I heard tell of a sett in a meadow they were once using but then left. A few years later, the field was ploughed and cropped. After several years, it was laid down to grass once more and, a couple of years after that, badgers returned to exactly the same spot and carried on as though they had never left.

It is marvellous how they find the old holes, but they have the best sense of smell of any animal I know and they follow ancient badger trails across the countryside. It may be a combination of these two things that enables them to return to a sett after a long period. If a wire fence is erected across one of their paths, they will tear a hole in it and keep doing so as fast as it is repaired rather than use a gate only a few years to one side. As regards their sense of smell, they will locate and dig down through more than a foot of soil to get at a nest of young rabbits so, all in all, the badger is a remarkable animal.

The rabbit too is a great survivor when you think about it. Not only does he have foxes, badgers, stoats and weasels prey-

ing on him, but also Man with all his inventive ideas, which include that terrible disease myxomatosis, but yet he keeps bouncing back. He is nature's way of providing for others because, without the rabbit, many predators would themselves find it hard to survive. Rabbits live quite happily in the bigger buries for most of the winter, but in early spring they breed. As their time comes near, the does go off on their own at night and dig a short single hole called a stop. She often chooses the middle of a field or some other isolated spot. When she has completed the hole, which is between six feet and ten feet in length and about six to ten inches deep, she collects dead grass to make a nest which she lines with fur scratched from her body. After she has given birth, she will feed her young and stop up the hole completely (hence the name 'stop') with soil when she leaves. When the young rabbits have their eyes open and need a bit more air, the doe partially fills the mouth of the hole. As soon as the young are running about, they are taken back to join the rest of the colony in the bigger buries. The doe goes off secretly to give birth because she knows full well that the old buck rabbit will often kill her young the moment they are born if she stays in the main bury.

I once saw a television programme about the rabbit and, during the programme, the commentator said that the adult rabbit was too big for a weasel to tackle. There are many keepers and countrymen who have seen a weasel kill a full grown hare! The weasel is a courageous little animal, living mostly on rats, mice, voles, rabbits and young song birds but he will have a go at almost anything if the opportunity arises. If you frighten a weasel off his kill he will come back and try to drag it away, sometimes coming almost up to your feet. He is also very inquisitive, which often leads to his undoing. If he is disturbed, he will run into cover and have a look at you from one place, run back and then have another peep from a different direction. Providing you stand quite still, he will have two or three looks at you before his curiosity is satisfied.

Nature is like a book. Once you have learned to read, you can begin to understand it. You have to think as the birds and animals do, learn their habits and what they like and dislike. Nature is perfectly honest in all her ways and there is a very good reason for everything that happens. If you take the opportunity to learn these things, there is pleasure in hearing the alarm call of a blackbird and seeing it flit from bush to bush along a hedgerow with his tail up straight. This usually means that a stoat, weasel or a cat is working along the other side. If a cock pheasant starts to call 'cock-up – cock-up', it means that he has seen a fox. Jays also will follow a predator through the wood sounding their alarm calls.

When I see people dressed identically in all the latest modern gear, rucksack on back, binoculars at the ready, trudging through the countryside going 'bird-watching', I often smile, for they see so very little. The best way is to find a patch of rough ground with a few bushes or a tree or two on it, back yourself into a hedge or a bush, wear dark clothes and sit on your backside keeping quiet and still. It is surprising what can be seen. I once sat with the local policeman on a small patch of rough ground and, in an hour and a half, we saw fourteen different species of birds and animals. As I sit at the window of my cottage writing these words, I can see from the window at this moment three different types of sparrows dusting them-selves; sitting on the weeds in the flower border is a pair of greenfinches; feeding on the grass under the ash tree seventy yards away is a pair of Canada geese which are nesting on the lake; in the tree is a pair of green woodpeckers, busy feeding their young and there is a pair of spotted fly-catchers gathering

insects from the lawn and taking them to their young in the nest in the climbing hydrangeas on the wall of my dog kennel.

Every year, we have sparrows nesting in our roof and their constant chattering usually wakes us early in the morning more efficiently than any alarm clock. Two years ago these sparrows vanished and we wondered what had become of them. A month or so later my wife found the answer, for she saw three young weasels sliding out of the down-pipe of the guttering. A bitch had reared her young ones in the roof and not one of us had seen any sign of her coming or going. I have known of several similar instances where weasels go up the inside of a down-pipe, appear in the guttering and from there vanish into the roof.

Most years in late August or September, a buzzard turns up at Tetworth. It does not stay long, about three weeks being average, but this year one came in late August and was still here in early June. I think the ones that visit us are young birds driven away by their parents which go for a journey around the country before returning south to find a mate; buzzards do not breed until they are two years old. The one that came this year took up residence in an oak on the edge of my rearing field and my son saw him most mornings, sitting on a dead branch at the top of the tree. He became so used to our comings and goings that he hardly bothered to take wing, provided we did not go too close. If we had a pheasant that had been damaged on a shooting day by falling into a bush or tree, or a rabbit caught by the dogs, we put it under his tree and he fed quite happily; perhaps that was why he stayed so long. It was lovely to watch him riding a thermal over the edge of the wood. Keepers tend to see birds of prey more than most folk because, when we are on the rearing field with our young pheasants or feeding them in the woods in the winter, we notice the birds turn their heads on one side and look up and, when we do the same, very often it is a hawk or a buzzard passing overhead, sometimes no more than a mere speck in the sky.

A question I am often asked is which season of the year do I like best, and the answer is that I like them all equally. In late January, February and March, there seems to be a sense of expectancy in the air with the birds and animals becoming more secretive in their behaviour and going through their early courtship displays, as though they feel they ought to start practising for the more serious business. When spring starts properly there is all the busy activity of 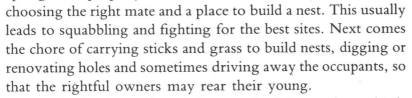 choosing the right mate and a place to build a nest. This usually leads to squabbling and fighting for the best sites. Next comes the chore of carrying sticks and grass to build nests, digging or renovating holes and sometimes driving away the occupants, so that the rightful owners may rear their young.

I wonder how many people have noticed that predatory birds and animals are always the first to have their families. The reason for this is that their young are growing and demanding more food at the very time of year when most food is available. Also, young foxes and stoats have to be taught by their parents to hunt and catch prey and, later in the year, there are plenty of young rabbits and young birds which are easy to catch, for them to practise on. Young birds and rabbits which manage to escape receive a sharp lesson in survival, for the experience teaches them to be on constant alert for danger.

During the summer months, there is a frenzy of activity, with parents of all kinds busy carrying food to their families and, as you walk through the woods, you see that the wild flowers have come once again and some of the rare species like the herb Paris or the butterfly orchid have multiplied since the year before. At that time of year, the rearing field is a busy

place, claiming most of the keeper's time for there is the daily round of collecting eggs, setting them in the incubators every few days, testing them for fertility, transferring them to a still-air machine and waiting anxiously for them to hatch. I am able to peep through a glass window in our incubators and see this happening. I remember how fascinated I was the first time I saw a chick emerge from the shell: I have seen many thousands hatch since and still the magic remains.

I try to find time in the evenings just to stand and watch young birds doing the things they like best, searching in the long grass for insects, dusting in a mole hill or chasing after moths. They consume a tremendous number of insects of one kind or another during a year. Time spent watching is time well spent because you can identify any birds that are not well and will be able to prevent an outbreak of disease before it gets started. For the first fourteen days, at night, we shut our chicks in a small hut and shelter unit with a Calor gas heater and later, if it is a fine night, they are allowed to sleep out under the stars. When I am on the rearing field at dusk, I often see a pair of woodcock roding; we have quite a few pairs that stay with us during the summer to breed.

The autumn too is a lovely time of the year. The birds and animals are now full grown and look very much like their parents and it is only by their different behaviour that they can be picked out from the adults. The leaves are gradually changing colour from day to day, each variety of tree different in hue from the others. Langlands Wood lies on a slope with a good mixture of hazel, maple, oak, beech and Scots pine and, when the leaves are changing colour, it makes a grand show when viewed from the hill a quarter of a mile away. Autumn is also the time of year to start feeding the outside woods, places where we have not released the reared birds. In this way, we can gather in any reared ones that have strayed from the main woods and through the standing corn. Rides have to be cut and straw bales that we carted round to each feeding place at harvest time broken open so that we can scatter the corn in the straw and keep the birds busy scratching. Many worms and other insects get under the straw, which thus serves a two-fold purpose for, when a bird is busy scratching for corn, it may uncover a choice worm or beetle which it really prefers.

Bill Dawes at Clarendon taught me to make feed rides as long as possible and I have always followed his advice having, over the years, found it more effective to scatter fifteen pounds of corn over perhaps four hundred yards of feed ride than put it down on a mere thirty yards as some folk do. One very good reason for feeding like this is that a few old, over-yeared pheasants often turn up when you start feeding; they are pugnacious and will drive the younger birds off the ride, particularly if it is short. Another is that, if you put your feed down in a small space and there are many birds concentrated there, they will clear up the  corn too quickly so that, if pheasants arrive on the feed ride late because they have come a long way, there will be no food left. If they return a few times and find there is nothing left for them, they will not bother to return but will find somewhere else to feed, which may well be over the boundary on your neighbour's ground. I believe in feeding my main woods twice a day. When I have fed the last ones at night, I sit and watch the birds feeding and it is surprising how late it is when some of the last ones come in; they invariably go onto the straw, if only for ten minutes, and scratch a few grains before they go up to roost.

It is very important, in a dry spell during autumn, to have a plentiful supply of water available. When I sit and watch my birds in the last half hour of daylight, most of them will go and drink and some of the very late arrivals that come in just at dusk will always do the same rather than feed before they hurry off to their roosting tree.

When winter arrives you see some lovely pictures of frost patterns on the grasses and bushes, particularly if there is a fog, when some of the scenes can be quite breathtaking. I remember one such morning several years ago when we had a very dense fog, almost a thin rain at dusk, and at about midnight a severe frost gripped. The next morning, I went into Weavely Wood; the fog had lifted and the frost on the bushes and trees looked most spectacular. Every pigeon in the wood was on the ground, unable to fly because, as they had roosted in the trees, the fog had wetted their feathers and the sharp frost had frozen their wings closed. The pigeons walked about under the trees for about two hours until it gradually turned a bit warmer, their feathers thawed out and they were able to fly again. This was the only time I had seen pigeons so badly affected, but the strange thing was that the pheasants were not bothered at all. The human being may be a very clever animal, but no one can paint, sculpt or carve such wonderful colours and intricate patterns as nature. When I am walking in the woods on mornings like this, I often think about the people scurrying from their centrally-heated homes to centrally-heated offices and what pleasures they are missing.

Every time we arrive at the feed ride, we whistle to let any pheasants that have strayed deep into the wood know that we are there with some food. The song birds quickly learn to associate the whistle with corn being scattered and they join in the feast. When we arrive at the feed ride, particularly if it is a cold, frosty morning with snow on the ground, we see the small birds sitting in the bushes and trees with their heads pulled deep into their shoulders and their feathers puffed out against the cold. Directly we start whistling, their heads pop out and they start twittering and chirping for all the world as though they were answering your whistle and, as you walk down the

ride, they flutter down from the trees and feed with the pheasants.

A few years ago, we had a heavy fall of snow and I was restricted as to where I could go, even with the Land-Rover, because of the deep drifts. On Sunday morning, there was a blizzard but I had managed to feed all the woods that morning except one which was isolated. The closest I could get with the Land-Rover was about a mile away so I set off to carry a side bag full of corn across the fields. It was a terrible journey; more often than not the snow was over my wellington-boot tops and up to my waist when the drifts gave way under me. Eventually I reached Kim's Spinney and saw all the pheasants and small birds waiting for me. I kicked a narrow path down the feed ride and, as I scattered the corn, both song birds and pheasants were feeding ravenously only a couple of feet from me, they were so hungry. I stood on one end of the ride watching them before starting my long trek back to the Land Rover, feeling that my effort had been worthwhile. I also remember wondering where all the conservationists were that morning. Most keepers like a fall of snow because it provides us with a wonderful opportunity to see, by means of tracks in the snow, just what is happening around us. You can see where a fox walked down the ride and suddenly jumped sideways to kill and eat a vole in a tussock protruding from the snow, or where a weasel has caught a small bird.

It is easy in any weather to tell a sparrowhawk kill, usually a pigeon, for you will find a small bunch of feathers where the pigeon first hit the ground and a trail of loose ones where it bounced along, a short distance away you will find the pigeon itself, lying on its back with its wings outstretched and perhaps one side of its breast eaten. When the hawk has eaten only half of the breast, he will often fly off and return later to the kill to finish the meal. If you take the trouble to examine the pigeon, you will find a small bald patch on its back where the talons struck. On a few occasions in my life, I have seen a hawk stoop and strike a pigeon or jackdaw, an awe-inspiring sight for the hawk swoops down from above his victim with his wings half closed, going like a bullet. When he strikes, usually just behind the pigeon's wings, you see a squirt of feathers and the bird falls from the sky dead. Sometimes the victim spots the hawk coming first and takes drastic avoiding action by making for the sanctuary of a tree. If he arrives there safely before his enemy can launch another attack, the hawk will usually fly around and swoop at the tree a few times, screaming like mad to frighten his prey out into the open, but the pigeon wisely stays where he is until the hawk finally gives up and flies off to look for an easier meal. A hawk will not fly into the branches to dislodge his prey for fear of damaging his wings.

The sparrowhawk makes most of his kills by flying at great speed low down alongside a hedge and every so often he whips over the hedge and catches a thrush or a blackbird which has not seen him coming. He employs a similar tactic in woods, flying down a ride and suddenly bursting into a clearing or turning sharply into another ride; if a small bird is slow in taking cover, that's usually his lot. For many years we had a pair of hobbies nesting at Tetworth, but I am sorry to say we have not seen them for two seasons now. They were often to be seen on a summer evening, hawking for dragonflies over the ponds.

Most birds of prey took a terrible beating years ago when highly toxic seed dressings were still legal. I was talking to a biologist from the Game Conservancy at the Game Fair at the time when predatory birds and some animals were dying at an alarming rate. He explained that the seed-eating birds, such as pigeons, feeding on the dressed corn, had to eat quite a lot before it killed them, but if a predator killed and ate one of these birds, or fed on the carcase of one that had already died, it ingested a large dose of poison at one go. Those seed dressings are not used any more and it is seldom we find any dead birds at drilling time like we did in those days.

I was feeding in Langlands Wood one morning, and snow was on the ground, when I saw a hare about two hundred yards away coming straight towards me. As he came closer I could tell by his manner that something was wrong with him. He passed close to me and, when I looked back the way he had come, I saw a stoat running his tracks like a retriever dog with his head and tail in the air. When the stoat was about twenty yards from me, I shouted and ran towards him. He stopped, looked at me, made a wide half circle and returned to the hare's tracks about thirty yards behind me and continued pursuit. Once a stoat has selected his victim, the only thing that will stop him is a charge of shot. The thing that amazes me when I see one after a hare is that the hare has ten times the speed of a stoat and can run very fast for a long time and could run miles away from the stoat in a few moments. However, the hare only travels at a slow lope with his ears laid back and the stoat keeps up his relentless pursuit until he finally kills his victim; he seldom misses.

Occasionally, when you pass a rabbit bury, a rabbit will bolt out of a hole, a sure sign that a stoat is working below ground. If you stand still, and if the wind is in your favour, you will see the stoat come out and scent around for a few seconds until he picks up the rabbit's trail and then sets off in pursuit. When snow is on the ground you can see most of the chase because the rabbit will not leave the wood but runs in a circle. As the rabbit

grows tired he runs in ever smaller circles and when he realises he cannot escape he will start to squeal. Shortly after this, he halts, completely exhausted, and the stoat will finish the job he started. When I was very young I was taught, when I heard a rabbit squeal, to count to ten and then get to the place as quickly as possible, because that rabbit would be one of the best rabbits on the bury and I would pick up a good dinner just before the stoat killed. A stoat never bothers with a sickly rabbit but selects only the best.

One of the less pleasant jobs a keeper does in the winter time is night-watching for poachers. There are some folk who look

upon poaching in the romantic kind of way described in the song 'The Lincolnshire Poacher', but in my book there is nothing romantic in shooting a roosting pheasant. A poacher is taking something that does not belong to him and that must be stealing. Years ago, when wages were very low and families were large, there may have been a genuine excuse for taking food for a starving family, but these days, with the modern standard of living, there is no such reason; it is done purely for monetary gain. These men go about in armed gangs and woe betide the keeper or any other person who stands up to them.

Night-watching is a cold lonely job and it helps to pass the time if you learn to identify some of the night sounds, like the rabbit squeal, suddenly cut off because he has fallen victim to a poaching cat or a fox. A lapwing flying and crying at night means a fox or a human being has disturbed him by walking across the fields where he is roosting. The lapwing is a very good friend and watchdog at night, who tells you where a person is and which way he is walking because he will follow whatever has disturbed him across the fields, giving his plaintive warning cry every few seconds. If you are standing on the downwind edge of a wood and you hear pigeons clattering out, it is a sure sign that someone is in there. If you see a pigeon fly into the wood you are waiting by, you suspect that the bird has been disturbed from the next wood in the direction from which he came. When out at night, particularly near Christmas, I have heard a vixen scream very close behind me in the wood, a most unearthly sound, and although I have experienced it many times it still makes the hackles rise on the back of my neck.

When I was at Clarendon Park, the poultry manager came to see me and asked if I would be doing any night-watching. I said I would and asked why he was interested. He told me that he was losing the occasional chicken, perhaps one a fortnight, and asked if I would mind keeping my eye on his birds when I was out. I told him I would do my best. That night, Bill Dawes and I took up a position from which we could keep watch on our own woods and also on the poultry houses. It was a lovely night, with a little wind and clouds scudding across the moon, and we waited until nearly two in the morning. Bill said, 'I don't think we shall have any company tonight, I'm off home'. Then he went across to one of the poultry houses, took out a chicken, wrung its neck and as he put it in his pocket remarked, 'I've got some company coming for Sunday lunch; goodnight, mate', and off he went. I expect that chicken probably joined the others that had gone missing.

There are some occasions when it is better to turn a blind eye if you discover you are losing the odd pheasant. One shooting day, by pure chance, I happened to count the birds we had shot just as the last drive had finished and not back at the Hall where I usually did it. After I had given the guns a brace each, I counted again and found I was one brace short. The next two occasions we shot, I checked most carefully and found I was missing a brace each day. I suspected that the birds were being hidden somewhere for collection later at night. I had a good idea who was responsible and, at the end of our following shoot, I managed to get away very quickly, took my dogs to where I thought the pheasants might be hidden and started working them. It was not very long before they found the birds

hidden under some leaves. My first reaction was to wait nearby and catch the man red-handed, but then I realised that, if I reported the matter, it would place my guv'nor in a very embarrassing situation because the person concerned worked for a very good friend of his. I did not know what to do, for I could not report what was going on, yet I had to put a stop to it. The man concerned was a very nice old boy with a wonderful sense of humour so I took the pheasants a little way off, plucked them, put them back where my dogs had found them and went home for my meal. I returned to the spot the next morning and the birds had gone. I remained good friends with that man for many years; as far as I know I never lost any more birds in that way and the matter was never mentioned between us. Thinking about this after, it would not have hurt the man to have left a note thanking me for plucking the pheasants and, knowing his sense of humour, I'm surprised he did not.

After having completed my morning feeding rounds, I was on my way home for lunch and, as I turned a corner in the road, I noticed a light lorry parked on the side. As I approached, the lorry started moving towards me and had barely picked up speed when I saw a cloud of smoke and dust burst from the door on the passengers side. This puzzled me as I could not imagine what could have caused it. A couple of days later I discovered the answer. A friend of mine explained that two men in the lorry had stopped to poach a pheasant. They had just loaded their old-fashioned hammer gun and were in the act of pushing it through the open window when they saw my Land Rover come round the corner. The loaded gun was rapidly withdrawn, placed across the seat and covered over with a sack. As they hurried off one of the passengers sat down violently on the weapon which promptly went off, blowing a hole through the door, thus explaining the smoke and dust that I had seen. It was more luck than they deserved that no one was seriously injured.

I went one afternoon to visit a good keeper friend of mine who looked after the Hazels Hall Estate, which is owned by the Rt Hon. Mr Francis Pym. Whilst there, I was introduced to Neil Day, who was to become a firm friend for twenty-four years. Since that far off day, we have spent a great deal of time in each other's company and never had a cross word. Shortly after I had met him, Neil called to see me at a time when I was recovering from an attack of bronchitis. He was very excited about going down to Christchurch in Hampshire the next day to fish the famous Bridge Pool for sea trout. My wife who often rushes in where angels fear to tread, God bless her, asked Neil if he would take me with him, partly because she felt it would do me good and partly to get me out of her way for a day. Neil, being the kind person he is, readily agreed, assured me that I would not be imposing and said he would be glad of my company on the long drive. I asked Rodney and Angela, who were not at school, to help my wife look after the rearing field.

At half past four next morning, we struck off for Christchurch. All the journey down, I was wondering how anyone could get so excited as Neil obviously was over a few fish. It was not to be very long before I found the answer and I was to become just as crazy about fishing the Bridge Pool as he was. We arrived safely and ate a good breakfast at the Station Café and started to fish, me doing the ghillie's job, netting the fish. After an hour or so, Neil struck into a six-pound sea trout and he immediately handed me the rod for me to play the fish. I protested that I would surely lose it, but he said, 'Well, if you do, we will try and catch another'. With a mere four-pound breaking strain line I played the fish for what seemed an eternity and finally got him to the net and triumphantly into the boat, where I was able to feast my eyes on a thing of rare beauty, a fresh-run sea trout, a bar of silver straight from the sea.

Later in the day, when I was fishing under instruction and caustic comments from Neil, I hooked and landed an even bigger one. I liked to think that I caught those two fish but, if I am honest, it was they who hooked me because, since that day twenty-four years ago, I have been privileged to fish the Bridge Pool on three or four days a year and I am still just as excited each time I go. A couple of years later, I met John Jacobs and his charming wife Rita, who have since become very dear friends. They live in the lovely New Forest town of Lyndhurst. John fishes with us and, when we go down to the Royalty Waters, we stay with them at the Stable Cottage and enjoy their generous hospitality. It is just like going home, the welcome is so warm; we are barely out of the car before a stiff whisky is thrust into our hands (no complaints) and, after a couple of these have helped us unwind from our journey, Rita is soon calling for us to come and enjoy one of her sumptuous meals. It is seldom she has to call twice. Rita listens once again to all our endless fishing stories and how we are going to fill the boat with fish the next day.

Whether it is hunting, shooting or fishing, there is a lot more to be had from your sports than actual participation. The excitement of getting ready to go, the wonderful people one meets, old friends to see again and yarns to be swopped – this, to me, is just as important as pulling a trigger. It is not just going, it is being invited to go. We would never dream of fishing the Royalty waters without taking time off at lunch time, even if the fish are taking like mad, to go up to the 'Surgery' (British Legion Club) and meet old friends, especially Ken Keynes and his brother Chubby. Ken is head bailiff and knows every nook and cranny of his lovely river, which he guards most jealously. At the same time, he is most helpful to anyone who has the good sense to seek his advice, which he gives most readily: what the fish are taking, the best type of fly or where there is a salmon lying which he thinks just might take. On more than one occasion, I have seen him patiently making sure that a young lad just starting out on his fishing career and trying to catch a few dace, has set up his tackle correctly. Like most sports professionals, nothing gives him more pleasure than to see someone he has helped benefit from his advice.

Several years ago, we had a wonderful day in the Bridge Pool; they are all wonderful days, of course, but on this particular one we had caught a number of sea trout from two to seven pounds and, when we came to pack up for the night, we discovered we had nothing to put the fish in. Neil had a brand new plastic mackintosh so we laid them on that. He gathered up the corners of the mac' and set across the road for the car, leaving us to bring the rest of the gear. A few seconds later, we heard car horns blowing and a lot of shouting from the road. I dashed up to see what was going on and saw Neil, in the middle of the road, frantically trying to scoop the fish back onto the mac and the drivers of the cars which had screeched to a halt were giving him some helpful advice on how to do it. What had happened was that, as Neil dashed across the road carrying the fish, the sleeve of the mac had slipped out of his hand and the fish slithered down the sleeve and out across the tarmac.

I was very fortunate the day I met John Jacobs, for not only has he shown great patience in improving my own golf game

but thanks to him I have been able to play with some of the top pros in the country and been introduced to a whole new world. I owe a great debt of gratitude to all those kind friends who have taken me fishing, shooting and golfing as their guest on so many occasions and I would never have been able to do many things without their generosity.

I mentioned previously that I had not seen the hobby hawks at Tetworth for two years. A week after writing those words I saw a young one at close range on two separate occasions. Whether it was the same one seen twice or two different ones I am not sure, but it is good to know they are still with us. We did have several pairs of nightingales when I first came to Tetworth but, over the years, they seem to have vanished. It is possible that we still have the odd pair, but I cannot hear them these days having grown rather deaf. I miss very much not being able to hear the twittering of the small song birds but I can still hear the chattering call of the magpie, the croak of a carrion crow and the crack of a poacher's .22 rifle.

A bird which heralds the approach of a bad winter is the fieldfare. When the flocks pass through Tetworth, ravenously feeding on the berries in larger numbers than usual, we may expect some harsh weather later on. On the other side of the coin, if the lapwings, which nest in the early spring, suddenly move off to the fens and the marsh counties, the weather often turns dry and warm. When we see them return, even if the weather may have been hot and dry for weeks, it will not be long before the spell breaks. We think we are very clever in the satellite age of weather forecasting but the birds and animals seem to know much more than we do.

Sir Peter and Lady Crossman have created a lovely garden at Tetworth, very much like the one at Clarendon Park but not quite as big. It has been designed around two ponds on two different levels, one being some fifteen feet higher than the other and up a steep slope. An enormous plane tree, the biggest I have ever seen, rears up on the south side and, if I stand on the bank under the plane in the spring, I can look down onto a kaleidoscopic blaze of different colours. Paths wind their way

through the gardens, but my favourite view of all is to walk along the top of the bank and look down from above. During spring and summer, Sir Peter and Lady Crossman spend every minute they can spare tending the garden. The guv'nor can usually be found by watching for his clouds of cigar smoke filtering through the blooms of a rhododendron to the accompaniment of a transistor radio, keeping him informed of events in the test match or golf tournament. I laughed heartily one morning last autumn as I walked through the gardens, having just fed the pheasants in The Larches. The governor had spent hours the day before, raking the indestructible leaves of the plane tree into heaps around the banks of the top pond. There were four or five heaps of leaves with a cock pheasant on the top of each one scratching away, scattering his carefully-raked leaves to the four winds.

# 6 · Foxes and Pheasants

**C**an hunting and shooting go together? This is a question which has created many arguments and about which much has been written. In my opinion, the two sports can and should go together. I believe that, whilst enjoying my own particular sport, I should try not to spoil that of other people. Unfortunately, there are quite a few folk who are only interested in either shooting or hunting and, if their interests are only in the one sport, they tend to regard the other as a nuisance, instead of seeking common ground. There are many ways one can go about this from the shooting side; the most important thing is that the estate owner with the sporting rights in hand, or the shooting tenant, makes it quite clear that he wishes the two sports to go along together. So many times have I heard a keeper spoken ill of when, after all, he is only an employee trying to carry out his employer's wishes.

Fortunately, here at Tetworth, I have the right sort of guv'nor who is always ready to indulge in my plans to try to improve the sport, schemes that usually end up costing him money, such as planting a new wood or making a cold and draughty wood warmer by planting a strip of canary grass down the windy side. I have never hesitated to release my reared birds into a wood where I know there is a litter of fox cubs. Knowing full well that they will kill a certain number of them, I try to cut the losses down to the minimum. When the poults are released, one of the most important things is to have a very large release pen. One of ours measures one hundred yards along each of its four sides and encloses plenty of ground cover for the poults to dive under if they are disturbed; their natural instinct is to hide if they are frightened in any way. Make the corners of the pen rounded and the birds will run round the corner and not congregate and panic one another.

Young pheasants make many short flights during the day, strengthening their wings, and if the pen is too small they just

fly straight out over the wire. I like to try and keep as many birds as possible in the pen for the first three or four weeks, after which I start letting them out. So many times have I looked at other Estates' release pens and thought them too small with little or no ground cover so that, if a fox or a dog walked down the outside of the wire netting frightening the poults, they would take wing and fly straight out the other side. When this happens they are at the mercy of anything, because a poult at that age can only make one good strong flight and cannot fly again properly until it has had a rest. This is one of the reasons why, when a fox or a dog puts up a young pheasant, it will watch it carefully until it settles and then run quickly to the spot; if they find that bird again, they can usually catch it quite easily.

We never clip our poults' wings because, if they get out of the pen in the early days of their release, as many of them do, they stand a better chance if they are full-winged. We make sure that we have a very good wire electric fence about eighteen inches from the outside of the pen. The bottom wire is about ten inches from ground level and the top one about one foot or so above that so that, if a fox or dog tries to dig under the wire netting or gets close enough to jump over the top, he must first make contact with the electric fence. If my dogs are anything to go by, once they have had this shock they will not go anywhere near the fence again. Over the last eight years or so, we have found it useful to set a fence of electrified sheep-netting about fiteen years away from the release pen. When this fence is first set up, the poults tend to run up and down it but they quickly learn to run through the large square mesh if they are frightened or disturbed back to the release pen as they associate the pen with home; this creates a safe area.

I know full well that, given half a chance, foxes are going to catch a certain number of my birds since that is their nature, but if this sort of precaution is taken and it saves a few birds, it makes the time and trouble all worthwhile. It is important to help young pheasants as much as possible during their first three to four weeks of release. Until then, they have led a sheltered life on the rearing field and have not been exposed to the dangers that they will encounter when they are taken to the woods. After four weeks, they should all be going up to roost at night and then seventy-
five percent of the danger will be over. It seems to me stupid to spend a great deal of time and money on rearing birds and then not to take sufficient care of them when they are taken to the woods. When shooting days prove disappointing, it is temptingly easy to lay the blame at someone else's door.

Some shooting people will not have the foxhounds in their covers until after they have finished shooting, believing that the hounds and general disturbance will drive their pheasants away. I have watched hounds drawing and running through my covers for twenty-five years and have no hesitation in saying that they do not upset or frighten pheasants in any way. In actual fact, the day after the hounds have been, I usually have a few more birds on the feed rides because the outlying birds down the hedgerows are driven home. Once I took Mr Nigel

Peel, MFH, when he was hunting the Cambridgeshire Fox-hounds, to see my birds on the feed ride, just an hour and a half after he had found a fox in that wood. He could not believe his eyes when he saw how many were feeding and how undisturbed they were. The only time hounds do upset pheasants is if the covers are drawn late in the day, just as birds are going up to roost, but the majority of Masters and huntsmen are aware of this and usually blow for home in ample time. Some people say that it is easy for me as I have a big estate, so that if birds leave one wood they can move to another, but, if birds leave the wood, they are just as likely to go over the boundary. We also have several small woods on our boundary and many is the time I have watched hounds running through these small woods and seen a few pheasants fly over the boundary, but I find they are usually back on the feed ride next morning. It is surprising how few pheasants are put on the wing by hounds when they are in a wood and only a very small percentage find it necessary to fly to get out of the way. If pheasants are in kale or game cover, where they have been attracted from the wood, and hounds go in, the majority of birds will fly back to the wood but will return to the cover very quickly and settle down within a few days. If asked, huntsmen will do their best to avoid these places. I have no doubt that my views on hunting and shooting on the same ground will cause comment but all I can offer in my defence is the opinion of the many people who have shot and/or hunted at Tetworth as guests of my employers.

One of the things I like about foxhunting is that, as I go about my normal duties in the autumn, I observe the signs that tell me that foxes are present in a certain wood, such as where one has eaten a pigeon or a rabbit, fresh droppings or pad marks or the 'cock-up' call of a cock pheasant during the day. If it is a young fox, you may spot him walking slowly across a ride, intent on what he is doing, or find where he has rolled in something nice and smelly. Vixens are more in the habit of doing this than dog foxes. Having informed the Master of where a fox is lying. I

like to estimate in which direction he will leave the cover. The wind plays an important part in making 'Charlie' decide which way to go. If there is little or no wind, he might go in any direction but if there is any breeze at all he nearly always goes into or across its direction. Some of the old foot-followers claim that he won't run downwind because the wind blows his brush and he can't turn very easily and these foot-followers are usually knowledgeable folk. The true reason a fox likes to run into or across the wind is so that he can wind or smell what is ahead of him. I position myself on the side of the wood I think he will leave and, if I get it right, I watch him go across country until he is out of sight; then I look back to where hounds are puzzling out the line of the scent. Sometimes, if the scent is a bit catchy, you will see first one hound pick up the line and drive forward giving tongue, only to falter after a short distance. Then another will pass the leader and pick up the trail and so they go on, with the leading hound forever changing places as first one and then another gets a whiff of scent.

Occasionally, on windy days, when the fox has run across the wind, the hounds may run as far as seventy yards on the

downwind side of the line that he has taken, catching the scent as it is blown down to them by the wind. They seldom run far under these conditions. When scenting conditions are reasonable and hounds run well, they often overshoot the line if the fox has turned sharply. Then it is lovely to watch hounds cast themselves across a field, trying to pick up the scent. Whereas before they were running in a tight pack, now they fan out across the field, turning in a big circle, each hound working individually. If you are lucky, you will see one or two hesitate at a spot, their sterns waving vigorously, which tells you they have found the place where the fox has turned. These hounds are often the older and wiser animals. They start to whimper a little and the rest of the pack, encouraged by the huntsman, will fly to them and, before long, they pick up the line and off they go again. This is the real pleasure of hunting for me: when I know that the fox is lying in a certain wood and have seen him go away across country and remembered exactly which line he has taken, and then have watched hounds come tumbling out of the wood, usually a long way behind, trying to follow that invisible line. Horses, hounds and people become very excited and the fox invariably gets clean away.

I often laugh when I see some of the older local foot followers who turn up at every meet, walking along very slowly often with the aid of a stick, complaining when asked how difficult it is for them to get about because of their bad backs and rheumatics. In spite of their ailments, they usually manage to get to each cover being drawn, even across a ploughed field, and, if the fox happens to cross the ride, they holler him over with great enthusiasm. If the fox goes away just round the corner of the wood from where they are standing, they dash like stags to watch the event, all traces of the 'screws' and bad backs quickly forgotten in the excitement. I have no doubt that, in years to come, I will become one of those old foot-followers standing at the covert side expounding my knowledge of the local foxes to anyone who is prepared to listen and to a good many folk who are not. A pack of fox hounds in full cry is a very exciting sound, very similar to the cry of the wild geese of my native Norfolk.

When I watch some of the people who ride to hounds I wonder where they find their pleasure for, when hounds are not actually running, most seem to spend their time gossiping. They never appear to watch the hounds working or take any interest in what the huntsman is trying to do so that, if I happen to arrive late and ask what has happened so far, I receive some very vague answers.

The fox is truly a very handsome animal when in his own environment, standing in a clearing in the wood with his front feet on a log or a mound of earth, the  autumn sun making his coat shine like silk, his ears pricked forward, intent only on whatever has attracted his attention and oblivious to everything else. At the same time, one must never underestimate his cunning; for all his good looks he is a ruthless killer if given half a chance. If a hen run is not shut securely at night or a pheasant release pen has fallen into disrepair, 'Charlie' will take full advantage of such an opportunity. Foxes have a wide and varied diet for, as well as eating all kinds of birds, animals and even earthworms, they also eat berries and fruit. Out of curiosity, I sometimes break their droppings open to see what they have been eating. Once I found in a dropping a dozen or more grains of dressed seed wheat, the first time that I have come across foxes eating corn.

Just before Christmas, the dog fox starts to call at night, giving a series of short barks as he is out on his rounds. This is the prelude to the mating season. The vixen usually starts calling just after Christmas and continues through January. When a vixen is in season she is often followed by several dog foxes and, if there happens to be snow on the ground at the time, people start writing to newspapers and magazines saying the foxes are so hungry they are hunting in packs! There is one thing those old dog foxes are hunting – and it is not food! On hunting days, the hounds will often draw blank good fox covers one after the other and then, in the most unlikely places, find three or more foxes lying together.

At this time of year, dog foxes travel long distances, a great deal further than we realise. It would be interesting to check through hunting records of the great runs by hounds before the days of the motorway. I would not mind betting that many of the long distance runs occurred at the end of January and during February and March, when the dog fox was far from his home territory in pursuit of a vixen and, if hounds found him, he decided discretion was the better part of valour and headed for home as fast as his legs would carry him. Dog foxes travelling miles to mate is probably nature's way of ensuring that fresh blood is introduced to prevent in-breeding. The act of mating between foxes is not often seen as it usually takes place at night or in the very early morning; I have seen it only three times in my life.

The vixen will often dig out more than one earth before she eventually decides to have her cubs in one of them. The reason for digging out two or three places is that sometimes she will have her cubs in one and later may move them to one of the others. It is easy to tell, apart from by the pad marks, if a fox or a badger has made the hole because a fox pulls the soil back quite a long way, very much as a rabbit does, but a badger heaps his spoil in a big mound. The dog fox does not play much part in the rearing of the cubs, but he will bring food to the vixen just after her young are born, when she cannot leave them; this only lasts for a few days, after which she does most of the work herself. If the dog fox happens to be near the breeding earth and he catches a rabbit or some other food, provided he is not hungry himself, he will carry it a little way from the earth and leave it for the vixen to take for the cubs, but after the first week he does not bother too much.

One of the things he will do, however, is bring moles and shrews. Why this should be I don't know and I would love to find the answer. The moles and shrews are not eaten but the vixen carries them to the earth and leaves them on the top of the ground. If you visit an earth often, you will see three or four moles lying about. I know that foxes love to roll in anything smelly, moles in particular, so is this one of the reasons? The dead moles in an earth usually look pretty well flattened. If any dead animal is left about at that time of the year, it is not long before the sexton beetle starts  to bury it and foxes love eating beetles, so they could be a useful source of food in that way. I have often found a litter of cubs I had no idea was in the vicinity, just by noticing a dead mole left on the edge of a ride or a path through the wood and coming back that way next day and finding it gone. Then I have hunted round and found the breeding earth not very far away, often in an old rabbit bury. I remember, one year at Clarendon, finding some cubs in an impenetrable place in a young forestry plantation heavily overgrown with brambles. I would never have discovered them had I not seen three different moles left on the centre ride over a period of a week, each of which had disappeared the next day.

As the cubs grow bigger and demand more and more food, the vixen can often be seen starting her hunting rounds much earlier in the day, particularly if she lives in a big wood. When the cubs are playing outside the earth in the evening sun, the vixen will approach upwind so that she can smell any danger and, if the coast is clear, she will give a low piercing whistle. The cubs stop their chasing immediately and rush to her, fighting one another to get the biggest share of the food. There is much spitting and snarling but seldom is any harm done and, once they have cleared up the food, like children the cubs quickly become friends again.

As the cubs grow older, they spend less time below ground living in the earth, particularly if it is in a wood where it is nice and quiet. They spend much time roaming around, stalking all kinds of prey without much success, but every so often they will come across something equally young and inexperienced, such as a young rabbit or a bird that has fallen from the nest, in which case they are able to grab an easy meal and learn something at the same time. They are also taking some of the workload from the vixen, all part of growing up which will stand them in good stead in later life.

I have often watched a cub in the late afternoon trying to catch one of my pheasant poults. He will step out onto the ride and see thirty or forty poults feeding on the straw ride. He drops to a crouching position and begins to stalk the poults, which see the cub as soon as he appears. All their heads go up

and they stand as high as possible, as though on tiptoe, with their necks craned towards the intruder. He creeps slowly towards the poults, taking advantage of every available piece of cover, until he considers he is close enough. Then he gathers his legs beneath him and springs forward like an arrow from the bow, only to find that the poults have flicked into the air and he passes harmlessly beneath them. After he has made a few of these headlong rushes and still not caught anything, he will give up in disgust, sit on his haunches in a lopsided kind of way and stare at the poults which, equally young and curious, gather round in a half circle about fifteen feet away, watching him intently. I liken the scene to the preacher addressing his flock. As time passes, the cubs are a little bit faster and more crafty and, if the poults grow more careless, as they often do, one of them comes to a sticky end, which makes the others treat the cubs with a greater respect in future. The cubs gradually become more independent of the vixen, and of one another, and start roaming further afield until early November when they disperse to take up a territory of their own.

When choosing a site for a release pen, it is worth bearing in mind that the first couple of times the woods are driven, the birds will usually fly back towards it. Thus it helps if you site your pen bearing in mind the way the woods can best be driven to show good sporting birds. If there are two woods with a gap of two or three hundred yards between, one can often show very good birds by feeding in the wood away from the pen in the morning to draw the birds away, and feeding in the wood with the pen in the afternoon, or *vice versa,* according to what time of day you want to shoot each particular place.

I am a strong believer in the use of sewelling to show sporting birds. Sewelling, for those folk who do not know, is a length of stout cord, some two hundred to three hundred yards long. We knot a piece of rag in the cord every ten inches and a very small bell every four or five yards. A track – the sewelling ride – is cut through the wood anywhere between twenty-five and thirty-five yards from the outside of the wood. We then push forked sticks into the ground every eight yards along the full length of the ride. The sewelling is run out and suspended in the forked sticks about eighteen inches off the ground. As the pheasants run down the wood, they fly when they get to the sewelling instead of when they reach the edge of the wood and are therefore much higher and more testing. It is worth bearing in mind that, by making the birds more testing, a greater percentage escape unscathed.

My aim when planning a drive is to put as many birds as possible over the guns and, at the same time, to make them fly a bit higher or curl on the wind so the guns cannot hit them. I do not recall a gun ever telling me he had had a good stand having shot 'X' number of birds, but dozens of times I have heard one say they were too difficult for him but grinning all over his face as he speaks. Sewelling does tend to turn a certain number of birds back over the beaters' heads, but both the governor and I are fully prepared to lose these birds as long as the ones that do go forward make more testing shots. Sewelling can be used to best advantage in a big wood where there is room for more than one drive or where there are two woods so close together that there is insufficient room between them for guns to stand far

enough back to give the pheasants a chance to gain height. If the birds are flushed fifty yards back in the wood, they fly over the tops of the trees as opposed to coming low out of the end of the wood and, having built up quite a bit of air speed, will often climb a bit higher still when they see the guns.

Mistakes are often made when it is decided to cut a sewelling ride by only looking at the matter from the guns' point of view. It is more important to design the drive from the pheasant's angle. It is no good cutting a path for the sewelling through a stand of tall ash or elm saplings and expect the pheasants to stand on the ride and take off vertically like skylarks. They like to take off gradually like an aircraft. If the trees or bushes in front are tall, I cut several narrow leads through to within a few yards of the outside of the wood, leaving a screen of saplings to make the birds fly over the top. These leads will also help to guide the birds in the direction I want them to go.

Several years ago, the wife of one of my oldest beaters said, 'I don't think Hickle will be able to come beating any more; his hip is getting so bad he can't walk very far'. Knowing how much he loved his beating I asked her to leave it with me and I would see if I could find something for him to do where little or no walking was involved. A few weeks later I called on Hickle and asked him if he would do me a favour and run the sewelling out and sit at one end and work it for me, explaining that it was not the straightforward job it looked; it needed someone with a bit of experience who knew what he was doing, otherwise we would have the birds rising in big flushes and going back over beaters' heads. Hickle readily agreed to have a go and did the job very well for several years. He grew so enthusiastic that my biggest problem was keeping him from making too much noise with his cries of, 'Over! Over!' or his audible comments when one of the guns missed a relatively simple shot.

One day, we were shooting Redgrass Wood behind my house. It is difficult wood to drive, but when things go right it produces some very sporting birds. We had driven the wood and reached the sewelling. It was a perfect day for this wood, with a stiff breeze making the birds fly high and curl on the wind, making very difficult shooting. I asked Hickle how the drive had gone he replied, 'Marvellous; there were a lovely lot of birds, they flew ever so well, but the guns could not hit them; all your work to get the birds here and then they missed most of them. I could have done better with my walking stick; they never should be allowed to come shooting if they can't shoot better than that', and with that off he stumped muttering away to himself and rolling up the sewelling as he went.

A fortnight later we were shooting Redgrass again. The drive went quite well, the majority of the birds flying forwards, getting up well over the trees. When we reached the sewelling, there was Hickle shaking his head muttering away. When I asked him what was wrong this time he said, 'They have killed too many; them guns never ought to be allowed to come shooting again; there ain't one of them that thought of leaving some for another day'. Then turning on his heel he pointed his walking stick straight at one of the guns, Danny Northrop, and said, 'You don't want that chap here again; he shot every pheasant that came over him; he's not missed one'. This just goes to show how much these old countrymen enjoy their sport and how seriously they take it, feeling very much a part of the occasion. Since those days, Hickle has had two hip operations and I see him out walking with his old pal on most days of the week. He is not able to come shooting any more, but every time the hounds meet locally he is very much in evidence, particularly on cubbing mornings.

Occasionally, a fox runs down towards the sewelling where a lot of birds may have concentrated. Providing I realise what has happened and see that the beaters give him a chance to find a way out, it is seldom that any harm is done. A little muntjac deer is another matter. It will charge up and down the sewelling ride, flushing birds in every direction, until it finally charges back past the beaters. The guv'nor and I have a very good understanding about foxes. If one will not leave the cover on hunting days, or upsets a drive on a shoot, it is always one of

Lady Crossman's foxes but if he breaks cover as soon as hounds enter and goes straight across country, giving hounds and riders a good run, then that fox is one of mine. When we were shooting in Weavely Wood a few years ago, I saw a fox stop and pick up a dead hen pheasant that the walking gun had just shot and run off with it, carrying it like a retriever. He was only twenty yards away from the beating line and although we gave him a good holler he refused to drop it. I am sure that fox too was one of Lady Crossman's!

I have a grand team of beaters here at Tetworth, every one of whom comes because he enjoys the day and many of whom have been coming every season for the twenty-five years I have been here. Loll Reynolds, who picks up for me, has only missed one shooting day in a quarter of a century: that was the day his father was buried and he still grumbles about missing the sport. When planning a pheasant drive in a very big wood, one must remember that the pheasants' last resort is their wings, their first instinct being to run, their second to try to hide and only if those fail do they fly. It would do all shooting people no harm if they worked a season as a  stop for they would learn what it is like from the keeper's point of view. Guns will stand gossiping instead of getting to their pegs and later they ask the keeper why the birds broke out at the side of the drive. Did the keeper think that he may have had the right-hand side of the beating line too far forward? They wonder why they get a grumpy reply.

When we are shooting Weaveley Wood, a hundred acres of thick cover, we have only three drives in any one day and sometimes only two. We blank the middle section to the outside sections and then we have some very good quality birds curling back over the guns to the centre of the wood, particularly if there is a strong wind. I like to have plenty of time for these blanking-in operations so that beaters may be lined out

down the ride and left standing for ten minutes or so. Then they start talking to one another and the mere sound of their voices is enough to make the birds run to the section of the wood where I want them. I always carry a bugle on shooting days and I blow a good blast to start the drive and another when it has finished. If I had it in my power, I would make it a rule that every keeper or person in charge of the day did the same for it makes life so much easier and more enjoyable for beaters, guns, pickers-up and everyone concerned. There is nothing worse than being left as a back gun or a picker-up deep in the wood and not knowing when the drive is starting or has finished.

Partridge days are my favourite. I enjoy planning the drives as I am going round the estate, feeding the pheasants in the woods and doing odd jobs, but at the same time keeping my eyes open for where the coveys are and where are the best hedges to put the birds over. I like to bring in fairly big tracts of land. That way I feel we do not damage the stock, since a partridge can only be driven so far before it will return to its home territory. By having the flankers well back, they are able to get behind the birds and push them into the middle of the drive. A covey will usually make one flight and then settle. The next time they fly must be over the guns, otherwise they are liable to break back over the beaters' heads, making for home territory. I am not keen on doing return drives where the partridges are mostly French because, if the ground is wet and heavy, as it is at Tetworth they run about so much they tire themselves out, cannot fly very well and do not make sporting shots. It is much better to give them an hour's rest or shoot that ground later in the day.

English partridges are entirely different because they go over the guns as a covey, instead of singly like the French birds, so you cannot hurt them by killing too many. The guns at best will shoot only one or two out of each covey and, by the time one has moved beaters round the back of them for a return drive, they have had a good rest and will fly as strongly as before. Also, the coveys which have flown on into the drive will give the fresh birds a lead back over the hedge.

The 'little brown birds', as partridges are often called, give most shooting people, guns, keepers and beaters alike, much more pleasure than pheasants. It may be because not only is the partridge a much more sporting bird but everyone can see every stage of drive, the flankers bringing the birds into the centre, where the partridge are settling. When they are flushed by the middle of the beating line, you can see how the flankers guide the covey over the guns, and hear the constant bawling of the keeper to 'Flag 'em up' on the right or left, whichever the case may be.

One of the keeper's headaches when trying to drive partridges over guns standing up close to a low hedge is the one or two guns that will persist in standing up straight, peering over the hedge and trying to see what is going on. These guns are invariably tall men with white, as opposed to weatherbeaten, faces, and wearing white shirts with their jackets unbuttoned so they can be seen for miles. It is very noticeable from the beating line how the partridges flying straight towards one of these guns suddenly turn and flare over the part of the hedge where there is a gun who has kept himself well hidden. What people ought to remember is that partridges do not sit out in the middle of the drive aimlessly doing nothing; they are on constant alert, looking for an escape route, well aware that the slow, steady approach of the white flags of the beaters spells danger. So, when they finally have to fly, they go over the hedge where the guns are hidden, carefully avoiding the man who is standing waist high above the hedge wondering why the birds are not coming over him.

I was talking about this with my governor one day and he said that guns standing up close to a low hedge ought to be made to carry a shooting stick and made to sit on it and I must say I agree with him. It is very frustrating indeed for keepers and beaters to walk a long way across fields, often heavy going, only to see their labours wasted by one or two guns who should know better.

Perhaps these guns are a bit like old George Timbers who worked at Sussex Farm many years ago. He was knocking and topping sugar beet one day, a back-breaking job as anyone who has ever done it will know. The foreman came into the field and George straightened his aching back and took out his ounce of Black Beauty Shag and started to roll a cigarette. The foreman, a devout Chapel man who detested smoking, said, 'George, if the good Lord had meant you to smoke, he would have put a chimney in the top of your head'. George thought for a few seconds before replying, 'That may be so, guv'nor, and if he had meant me to bend down like this, knocking and topping your bloody sugar beet, he would have put a hinge in me back'.

# Postscript

Agamekeeper's life is an ideal one, with the unique opportunity of observing nature more closely than almost anyone else; I see and learn something new every day. It is a way of life which demands total dedication but there are ample rewards. I have enjoyed writing this book and recalling days gone by, but I feel it is time now to draw to a close. I have led a wonderful life and been privilege to meet many delightful people, whose friendship I treasure. I spend my life doing what I love best, being a gamekeeper living with nature and, what is more, being paid to do it. Not many folk are so fortunate.

Before I blow the bugle for the finish of the last drive, may I pay tribute to Audrey for being the perfect keeper's wife. I could not have managed without her. I thank my employers, Sir Joseph Nickerson, the late Major Christie Miller and, in particular, Sir Peter and Lady Crossman who, for the last twenty-five years, have given me the opportunity to live the life I love. They own Tetworth Hall Estate, but there are often times when I think the woods and their occupants belong to me.